Copyright © 2025 The Grove Church

ISBN: 9798303921061

Scriptures taken from the Holy Bible, New International Version®, NIV®. Copyright © 1973, 1978, 1984, 2011 by Biblica, Inc.™ Used by permission of Zondervan. All rights reserved worldwide. www.zondervan.com The "NIV" and "New International Version" are trademarks registered in the United States Patent and Trademark Office by Biblica, Inc.™

Written by: Evan Westerfield, Aaron Denn, Nik Baumgart, and Hunter Shaw
Special thanks to our editors: Anna Ahlbrecht, Christin Rude and Kathy Ramsay
Photography: Ashlee Westerfield
Design: Emily Farmer, Eli Angulo, and Kelsey Shaw

The Grove Church
4705 Grove St
Marysville, WA 98270

www.grove.church | @thegrovech
info@grove.church
(360) 659-2276

THIS BELONGS TO:

_____

HOW TO USE THIS MAGAZINE

DON'T FORGET TO FILL IN THE ___BLANK___

| WIDE MARGINS FOR YOUR PERSONAL NOTES OR QUESTIONS

BESIDES 'FILL IN THE BLANKS', YOU'LL BE PROMPTED TO WRITE ABOUT YOUR OWN EXPERIENCES (DON'T WORRY, YOU DON'T HAVE TO SHARE THEM WITH ANYONE ELSE).

THIS IS YOUR MAGAZINE. MARK IT UP, TREAT IT LIKE A BOOKLET, ENGAGE WITH IT HOW YOU LIKE. THANK YOU FOR TAKING THESE NEXT STEPS IN YOUR WALK WITH CHRIST. THE GROVE CHURCH IS HONORED TO WALK ALONGSIDE YOU.

USE YOUR CAMERA APP TO SCAN THE QR CODE OR TYPE IN THE URL YOURSELF!

WWW.GROVE.CHURCH/HOW-TO-STUDY-THE-BIBLE-CLASS

| P.S. YOU'LL FIND MORE BLANK NOTE PAGES AT THE END!

TABLE OF CONTENTS

INTRODUCTION 009

EXPLORE > 015

017 **EXPLORE: WHO WE ARE**
027 **SALVATION**
029 **BAPTISM**
033 **COMMIT TO DAILY PRAYER**
039 **JOIN A LIFE GROUP**
043 **WHAT WE BELIEVE**
061 **HOW TO STUDY THE BIBLE**
085 **YOUVERSION BIBLE APP**
087 **WHICH BIBLE IS BEST FOR YOU?**
089 **JOIN A BIBLE READING PLAN**
091 **WORSHIP**

LEAD » 133

135 LEAD: WORKING TOGETHER TO ACCOMPLISH GOD'S MISSION
141 MEMBERSHIP
147 BUSINESS MEETING
149 SHARE YOUR FAITH
151 HOW TO LEAD
157 JOIN A MISSIONS TEAM

ENGAGE » 095

097 ENGAGE: USING WHO YOU ARE FOR GOD'S MISSION
107 LIVING GENEROUSLY
111 PRAYER AND FASTING
115 FIND YOUR TEAM
119 HOW YOU'RE WIRED
129 FINANCIAL PEACE UNIVERSITY

NEXT STEPS

CHECK THEM OFF AS YOU GO!

- ☐ SALVATION
- ☐ BAPTISM
- ☐ COMMIT TO DAILY PRAYER
- ☐ JOIN A LIFE GROUP
- ☐ JOIN BIBLE READING PLAN
- ☐ WORSHIP PLAYLIST
- ☐ LIVING GENEROUSLY
- ☐ PRAYER & FASTING
- ☐ FIND YOUR TEAM
- ☐ HOW YOU'RE WIRED
- ☐ FINANCIAL PEACE UNIVERSITY
- ☐ JOIN MEMBERSHIP
- ☐ ANNUAL BUSINESS MEETING
- ☐ SHARE YOUR FAITH
- ☐ JOIN A MISSIONS TEAM

EXPLORE
ENGAGE
LEAD
NIGHTS

SCAN TO SIGN UP!

OR VISIT: GROVE.CHURCH/EXPLORE-ENGAGE-LEAD-NIGHTS

In our Road Map to Christian Maturity you may see that we've broken all of our next steps down into three sections called Explore, Engage, and Lead. Each of these sections also starts with a class. The goal for you is to take each class, and in the months in between take some next steps found in each of the sections. If you're new to the church and take the Explore class, maybe join a Life Group and take the What We Believe Class before you take the Engage class.

> At our Explore → Engage → Lead Nights all three classes will be offered—but before everyone is dismissed to their class—we will eat together and get to know other people at the church, all in different steps of their journey.

We would love for you to join us at these events. Feel free to look at the rest of this magazine to see what other steps we have along the way. Our hope is that as you complete this magazine, you will find an even deeper relationship with Jesus.

LETTER FROM PASTOR NIK

Everybody has their "first time" in church. For some it's as a small child. For others it's as a kid or teenager, and still others as an adult. For many this is the beginning of their journey with Christ. The general idea in this phase is that they're not incredibly familiar with the Christian Faith, the Bible, Jesus, and a host of other spiritual and/or church-related things. They're "new."

Now picture a pastor, a board member, or someone who's been part of the Christian Faith for 10, 20, or 30+ years. While it's not assumed for everybody, many of those individuals have a greater understanding of their faith, Christlikeness, and maturity. They've introduced regular habits/disciplines into their lives like worship, prayer, Bible study. They've proven themselves faithful and are easily looked to for guidance from novices in the faith. These people are in key teaching, leadership and decision-making roles for all ages in the church. They're not perfect, but they're a long way down the road to becoming like Jesus.

Above is a picture of two people on opposite ends of the spectrum of Christian maturity. And there's everything in between, which means we're all in there somewhere! In a perfect world, no matter where we appear on the spectrum, we're moving in the direction of Christlikeness (maturity).

That's what the magazine is all about! As a team we've taken it upon ourselves to work on a pathway that will challenge, enlighten, and help everyone take steps toward Jesus. Throughout this magazine you'll find articles, links, classes offered—both in person and online—fill in the blank pages, and more. While working through everything in this magazine may take time, our hope and prayer is that you enjoy the journey; that you grow, experience transformation, enjoy connecting with others, and become more like Jesus.

Finally, I'm praying for you to have a stirring experience with the Holy Spirit and a growing hunger for certain disciplines that will help you in every way. Whether you're super new to the journey, somewhere in the middle, or well along on the path, I believe the tools in this magazine will help you immensely. If you're a parent, you'll be better equipped. If you're a student, through a Christ-centered lens. As an employee or boss or entrepreneur, humbly doing it all through Jesus. I'm praying you'd see everything you do through the lens of your growing faith.

The result of all of us taking steps on the journey is a healthy church that continues to reach a world desperately in need of a Savior!

LET'S DO THIS!

— Pastor Nik

THE CODE
LEARNING

We will admit that we don't know everything.

We will take risks, try new things, pray hard, and learn as we go.

EXPLORE THE CODE 013

SECTION ONE
EXPLORE>

EXPLORE | CLASS ONE

EXPLORE: WHO WE ARE

SCAN TO SIGN UP!
OR VISIT: GROVE.CHURCH/EXPLORE-ENGAGE-LEAD-NIGHTS

THIS IS THE FIRST PHASE IN OUR PATH TO CHRISTIAN MATURITY.

If you have been attending the church for any amount of time and are considering making the Grove Church your home church, then this is a great next step.

The Explore class is part of our quarterly Explore → Engage → Lead nights. When you attend you will have dinner with everyone attending that event, and then break off for the Explore class. In this class we will go over our history as a church, what we're all about, and what some next steps for you may be.

WE HOPE YOU'LL JOIN US AND TAKE THIS FIRST STEP!

EXPLORE
WHO WE ARE

CHURCH HISTORY

Our church has been here for over _____ years. It was first founded in 1932, and located by the Dairy Queen on 4th Street. In 1964, we moved into this building and have been adding on over the years.

OUR FIRST CHURCH BUILDING!

OUR CHURCH 90+ YEARS LATER!

In 2009, Nik took over as our lead pastor. As we began to drill down into what we wanted to be as a church, we arrived at _____

BELONGING

That word was _____. We wanted to create a church where no matter where you were on your faith journey, you could feel like you belong here. This leads to having a really _____ group of people attending, and we love that!

- People from birth to 100.
- People born and raised in Marysville, and people from all over the world.
- People who have a lot or a little.
- People who have been Christians for decades, and people who are just now checking out faith in Christ.

We ought to be a church where all can find their place, to _____ to the family and grow in Christ; where all can join a common mission.

This is an idea based in Scripture. In _____, as Paul is explaining the idea of no longer being under the Old Covenant, but the New Covenant of Christ, he proclaims:

> [25] Now that this faith has come, we are no longer under a guardian. [26] So in Christ Jesus you are all children of God through faith, [27] for all of you who were baptized into Christ have clothed yourselves with Christ. [28] There is neither Jew nor Gentile, neither slave nor free, nor is there male and female, for you are all one in Christ Jesus.
>
> (Galatians 3:25-28)

Or in Revelation, John sees a vision of Heaven:

> [9] After this I looked, and there before me was a great multitude that no one could count, _____, tribe, people and language, standing before the throne and before the Lamb. They were wearing white robes and were holding palm branches in their hands. [10] And they cried out in a loud voice: "Salvation belongs to our God, who sits on the throne, and to the Lamb."
>
> (Revelation 7:9-10)

Which leads us to...

OUR MISSION

LOVE GOD.
CONNECT WITH EACH OTHER.
SERVE ALL.

LOVE. CO

OUR MISSION

We've boiled down our mission as a church to three simple phrases: *Love God. Connect with Each Other. Serve All.*

Our mission as a church is to help people do each of these in the most _____ and _____ way possible.

LOVE GOD

For our first phrase, we say love God. This is a very _____ statement on purpose.

We can turn to Mark 12, to see how this can play out. When Jesus is asked what the most important commandment in the Law is, he responds this way:

> "29 The most important one," answered Jesus, "is this: 'Hear, O Israel: The Lord our God, the Lord is one. 30 _____ the Lord your God with all your heart and with all your soul and with all your mind and with all your strength.'
>
> (Mark 12:29-30)

So we strive to love God with _____ . It is right to feel the emotion of what God has done for us. To strive for and live a Holy life in gratitude to Him. To earnestly seek to learn more and more about who He is. To use our strength and talents to further _____ as much as possible.

This statement _____ the other two. We want to build healthy relationships because that is what God does for us. We want to serve others because that is what God does for us.

CONNECT WITH EACH OTHER

Our second phrase is "Connect with each other", and by this we mean that we want to live in authentic Christian _____. That may sound a little Christianese, but essentially this boils down to encouraging one another in Christ and to help one another grow in our relationship with God.

I love the way Paul says it in his letter to the church in Colossae:

> 12 Therefore, as God's _____ people, holy and dearly loved, clothe yourselves with compassion, kindness, humility, gentleness and patience. 13 Bear with each other and forgive one another if any of you has a grievance against someone. Forgive as the Lord forgave you. 14 And over all these virtues put on love, which binds them all together in _____.
>
> (Colossians 3:12-14)

SERVE ALL

Our final phrase is one that perhaps we are most known for in our community, and we strive for that to be so. We say "serve all." By this we mean that we strive to put our faith in Christ into _____. It's not enough for us to just accept the truth of what Jesus accomplished for us; we must show that love to others. Oftentimes the best way we've found is tangible work.

We can think about Paul reminding the church in Corinth as they bragged about knowing there was no sin in eating food offered to idols that "'We all possess knowledge." But knowledge _____ up, but love _____ up.' (1 Corinthians 8:1b). We can have all of the knowledge we want, but if we don't pair that with love, then it's worth nothing.

We love to create opportunities throughout the year for us to serve. We want to serve and love our _____, and for Scriptural background all we have to do is go back to that passage in Mark and read the next verse. After Jesus shared what He said the greatest commandment was, he shares the second greatest:

> [31] *The second is this: 'Love your neighbor as _____.' There is no commandment greater than these."*
>
> (Mark 12:31)

THE CODE

So if this is our mission and vision as a church, we call the next step in who we are our code. We believe that these 9 statements sum up who we to be as a church:

PASSION

We are passionate people. We will honor God with all in, faith.

GENEROUS

We will lead the way with generosity. We believe it is more blessed to give than to receive.

AUTHENTIC

We are real people challenging real people. We are easy to be around and dedicated to together.

SERIOUS

We are serious about the saving work of Jesus Christ. We know the methods will change but the never will.

LEARNING

We will admit that we don't know everything. We will take risks, try new things, pray hard, and as we go.

REACHING

We will do anything to reach people who don't know Christ.

FUN

We will laugh hard, loud, and often. Nothing is more fun than serving God with people you .

INTEGRITY

We will have character. We believe integrity is everything. Without it, nothing else matters.

SACRIFICE

We give up things we love for things we love even more. The church does not exist for . We are the church and we exist for the .

GOVERNANCE

Our next topic is going over what our _____ looks like as a Church. This may not be the most exciting topic, but it's an important topic to cover.

ASSEMBLIES OF GOD NETWORK LEADERSHIP

The network leadership is the governing body over all Assemblies of God _____ in Washington and northern Idaho.

STAFF

The staff works under the authority of the lead pastor and serves the _____ through particular job roles.

LEAD PASTOR

The lead pastor is the leader of our _____ in particular.

DEACON BOARD

The deacon board is a lay person (non-pastor) board made up of church members to _____ as accountability to the church.

OUR NEXT STEPS

Our church will be _____ years old in 2032. So it's often on our minds, "where do we want to be at 100?" Our vision is always how we can _____ our community. God has called us to Marysville, and we believe that we can make a difference not just here, but all around us.

- We want to plant churches in the communities around us.
- We want to continue to find ways to tangibly help our community through programs like iheart, Back to School Bash, Grove Tutoring, Carnival, and whatever else may arise.
- We want to make sure that the people in our church are constantly growing in their relationships with Christ. We want to make disciples of Jesus.
- We want to make an impact in the world through our giving and sending teams to accomplish missions work in other countries.
- And so much more.

YOUR NEXT STEPS

The next class in your path to Christian maturity is the Engage Class, which will be available in the next three to six months. In the meantime, we would highly recommend taking at least _____ steps located in section 1 of your Next Steps Book.

NEXT STEPS

SALVATION

All right, this is the big one. Every aspect of your Christian walk flows out from this step. The first idea that we need to take is that we are all sinful, every last one of us. Paul sums it up nicely when he says in his letter to the Roman church: *"for all have sinned and fall short of the glory of God"* (Romans 3:23). All of us were dead in our own sin, and without hope for eternal salvation. That is, until Jesus made a way! Jesus Christ is God in the flesh. He came to earth and lived among us. He lived the perfect sinless life that we could never live, He died the death that we deserved to die due to our sin, and He rose again showing that He had conquered sin and death. Because of what Jesus accomplished, we can have our relationship with God restored.

So how can we be saved? Well once again we can look to Paul's letter to the church in Rome where he says: "If you declare with your mouth, 'Jesus is Lord', and believe in your heart that God raised him from the dead, you will be saved." (Romans 10:9). We declare that Jesus is the Lord of all, and we believe that He truly did rise from the dead.

When we speak about salvation, there are two different aspects that we refer to. The first is called Justification. This is the idea that upon salvation, we are justified before God. We will get to enjoy eternity with Him, as we will no longer be judged for our own sin, but rather for what Christ has accomplished. The second aspect is called Sanctification. By this we mean the process of becoming more and more like Christ. In other words, part of salvation is the Holy Spirit working in our lives to help us live holy lives. James, Jesus' brother, puts it succinctly in his letter to the church in his day: *"In the same way, faith by itself, if it is not accompanied by action, is dead."* (James 2:17). In other words, our faith in Christ will always be accompanied by good works. This doesn't mean that we are now perfect and never sin, of course we all stumble and fall. It does mean that we are striving to live righteously, not to earn our salvation, but out of gratitude for our salvation.

If you are already a Christian, take a moment to share your story below. If you are not yet a Christian and would like to take that step, you can pray on your own right now! Confess that Jesus is Lord over all, and thank God for his gift of salvation. If you have taken this step we would love to speak with you. You can scan the QR code on the next page to make an appointment to speak with a pastor.

SCAN ME!

OR VISIT: GROVE.CHURCH/SALVATION

**HAVE YOU GIVEN YOUR LIFE TO CHRIST?
IF SO, SHARE YOUR TESTIMONY HERE:**

**IF YOU HAVEN'T TAKEN THAT STEP YET AND WOULD
LIKE TO, WE WOULD LOVE TO TALK WITH YOU.**

NEXT STEPS

BAPTISM

Baptism is one of the core sacraments (official ceremonial function) of the Church. We believe that baptism symbolizes our own dying to sin and rising again with Christ. In the Gospels, we see Baptism used by both John the Baptist and Jesus as a means of repentance of sin, and accepting the message of Christ.

In the book of Acts, we see that whenever someone makes a first time proclamation of faith in Christ, it is accompanied by baptism. So for us today we believe that when we become Christians, when we profess faith in Christ for the first time, the next Biblical step is to be baptized.

> *As they traveled along the road, they came to some water and the eunuch said, "Look, here is water. What can stand in the way of my being baptized?" And he gave orders to stop the chariot. Then both Philip and the eunuch went down into the water and Philip baptized him.*
>
> (Acts 8:36-38)

If you are a Christian, and have not yet been water baptized, scan the QR code to sign up! If you have been baptized, please share your experience.

SCAN ME!

OR VISIT: **GROVE.CHURCH/BAPTISM**

HAVE YOU BEEN BAPTIZED? SHARE YOUR STORY HERE:

THE CODE
PASSION

We are passionate people.

We will honor God with all in, risk-taking faith.

EXPLORE THE CODE 031

NEXT STEPS
COMMIT TO DAILY PRAYER

Consistent prayer is key for any healthy relationship with God. I once heard a pastor put it this way: "Would you believe me if I said I had a healthy relationship with my wife, and also said we hadn't spoken in a month?" Of course not!

> Prayer is simply speaking to God, and there is a lot involved in that.

One pitfall that we as Christians can fall into is making prayer about us, and we must fight against that. We cannot view God the way we may have viewed Santa Claus as a kid, someone to interact with only when we want something. Prayer should be authentic, vulnerable, and consistent. There is no one right way to pray, but let's take a look at the main example that Jesus Himself gives us:

> "This, then, is how you should pray:
> "'Our Father in heaven,
> hallowed be your name,
> your kingdom come,
> your will be done,
>   on earth as it is in heaven.
> Give us today our daily bread.
> And forgive us our debts,
>   as we also have forgiven our debtors.
> And lead us not into temptation,
>   but deliver us from the evil one.
>
> (Matthew 6:9-13)

Again, this is not to say that the only way to pray is by using the Lord's Prayer, but it does give us a helpful outline. When you pray through the Lord's Prayer, consider putting it into your own words and making it personal for you.

LET'S GO STEP BY STEP THROUGH THE PRAYER:

OUR FATHER IN HEAVEN, HALLOWED BE YOUR NAME.

So the first aspect of this prayer is to address God the Father, and recognize that He and His name are holy (set apart from everything else). It is good to start our prayer by putting our hearts in a humble posture before God.

YOUR KINGDOM COME, YOUR WILL BE DONE, ON EARTH AS IT IS IN HEAVEN.

This next aspect is again focused on God rather than ourselves. First, we praise God for who He is, and now we are praying that His plan and purpose would be accomplished here on Earth. Ultimately our chief desire should be that we can see God's perfect will accomplished, and that we would be used for this.

GIVE US TODAY OUR DAILY BREAD.

Here is the first part of the prayer where we bring up ourselves. It is good and right that we ask God for what we need, this is the idea of daily bread. We can bring our needs before the Lord, and ask that He provide them.

AND FORGIVE US OUR DEBTS, AS WE ALSO HAVE FORGIVEN OUR DEBTORS.

Here we bring our sin before the Lord and ask for forgiveness. This is not a moment to feel condemnation, but rather to express our sorrow for the ways in which we fall short, and also marvel at the beauty of God's forgiveness for us. In addition, we must remember to forgive those who sin against us. It would be an incredibly wicked thing to ask God for His forgiveness and not offer that forgiveness to others.

AND LEAD US NOT INTO TEMPTATION, BUT DELIVER US FROM THE EVIL ONE.

The final point of this prayer is asking the Lord for the help we need to pursue a Godly life. We can ask God for help in the midst of temptation and that He would protect us from the attacks of Satan.

DAILY COMMITMENT PRAYER SHEET

1	2	3	4	5	6	7	8	9	10
11	12	13	14	15	16	17	18	19	20
21	22	23	24	25	26	27	28	29	30
31	32	33	34	35	36	37	38	39	40
41	42	43	44	45	46	47	48	49	50
51	52	53	54	55	56	57	58	59	60

IT TAKES ABOUT 60 DAYS TO FORM A CONSISTENT HABIT. CHECK EVERYDAY AS YOU PRAY.

WHAT TIME WILL YOU BE PRAYING?

_____ AM/PM

WHERE WILL YOU BE PRAYING?

_____

EXPLORE
PRAYER

GROVE TUTORING

Do you or a student you know need a little extra help with school? If so, we offer free tutoring every week during the school year for 6-12 grade students. This is open to the whole community, not just those in our church. While there is no cost, pre-registration is required so please sign up at **grove.church/tutoring**

We could also always use more tutors to help with the growing number of students that we have attending. If you would be able to help with this, you can sign up to join at **grove.church/find-your-team**

SCAN TO PRE-REGISTER!

OR VISIT: GROVE.CHURCH/TUTORING

NEXT STEPS

JOIN A LIFE GROUP

Here's a simple truth, we are not meant to be alone. In the same way, we are not meant to be alone in our Christian journey.

> **Jesus established His Church so that we can pursue relationship with God together.**

One of the best ways to get connected with other people at the Grove is by joining a Life Group. In a Life Group you can meet weekly with other people in the church in a local home, have dinner, pray for each other, and study the Bible together.

To sign up for a Life Group, or to see more information about different Life Groups, scan the QR Code below.

SCAN ME!

OR VISIT: GROVE.CHURCH/LIFEGROUP-SIGN-UP

AFTER FINISHING A SESSION OF A LIFE GROUP, WRITE ABOUT YOUR EXPERIENCE BELOW:

THE CODE

AUTHENTIC

We are real people challenging real people.

We are easy to be around and dedicated to growing together.

EXPLORE THE CODE 041

EXPLORE | CLASS TWO

WHAT WE BELIEVE

SCAN TO SIGN UP!
OR VISIT: GROVE.CHURCH/WHAT-WE-BELIEVE

SO WHAT EXACTLY DOES IT MEAN TO BE A CHRISTIAN? WHAT DO WE BELIEVE AS A CHURCH?

Find out in the 3 week long **What We Believe** class where we will go over our statement of faith as a church, with Biblical backing for each point. Whether you are new to faith and wondering what exactly we believe as Christians, or have been a Christian for decades and want to learn more about basic doctrine, this is a great step to take.

WEEK 1:
ONE GOD, THE FALL, JESUS CHRIST,
THE CHURCH, COMMUNION AND BAPTISM

WEEK 2:
HEALING, THE RETURN OF CHRIST,
THE BIBLE, THE HOLY SPIRIT, MARRIAGE

WEEK 3:
THE CHURCH AND IT'S FUNCTIONS

EXPLORE
WHAT WE BELIEVE

WK 1: WHO GOD IS
— ONE GOD, JESUS CHRIST, THE HOLY SPIRT

ONE GOD

We believe there is an all-powerful and all-knowing God that loves mankind and displays that love through the work of the Holy Spirit and the Sacrifice of Jesus Christ for our sins.

> **We believe this one God exists in three distinct persons: God the Father, God the Son, and God the Holy Spirit.**

"We believe there is an all-powerful..." (omnipotent). We mean by this that God is able to do _____ that is logically possible and consistent with His character. This refutes _____ statements like "Can God create something more powerful than Himself?". It also refutes the assertion that if God cannot sin, then He is not all-powerful.

> So Sarah laughed to herself as she thought, "After I am worn out and my lord is old, will I now have this pleasure?" Then the Lord said to Abraham, "Why did Sarah laugh and say, 'Will I really have a child, now that I am old?' Is _____ too hard for the Lord? I will return to you at the appointed time next year, and Sarah will have a son."
>
> (Genesis 18:12-14)

"...and all-knowing God..." (omniscient). We mean by this that God knows all things, both what can _____ and _____ be.

> Nothing in all creation is _____ from God's sight. Everything is uncovered and laid bare before the eyes of him to whom we must give account.
>
> (Hebrews 4:13)

"...that loves mankind and displays that love through the work of the Holy Spirit and the Sacrifice of Jesus Christ for our sins." God did not simply create humanity as an experiment to discard, He loves us in a way even deeper than a _____loves their _____. God_____His love for us through the death and resurrection of Jesus for the forgiveness of our sins, and the active work of the Holy Spirit in our lives today.

> *But God demonstrates his own love for us in this: While we were _____, Christ died for us.*
>
> (Romans 5:8)

"We believe this one God exists in three distinct persons: God the Father, God the Son, and God the Holy Spirit." This is one of the most difficult Christian doctrines for us to comprehend. To put it simply, God exists in a way that is _____our understanding. There is One God, whose name is Yahweh (YHWH, LORD). This God exists as_____persons: The Father, the Son, and the Holy Spirit.

> *Then God said, "Let us make mankind in our image, in our likeness, so that they may rule over the fish in the sea and the birds in the sky, over the livestock and all the wild animals, and over all the creatures that move along the ground."*
>
> (Genesis 1:26)

> *In the beginning was the Word, and the Word was with God, and the Word_____.*
>
> (John 1:1)

> *Then Peter said, "Ananias, how is it that Satan has so filled your heart that you have lied to the_____and have kept for yourself some of the money you received for the land? Didn't it belong to you before it was sold? And after it was sold, wasn't the money at your disposal? What made you think of doing such a thing? You have not lied just to human beings but to_____."*
>
> (Acts 5:3-4)

EXPLORE >> WHAT WE BELIEVE

JESUS CHRIST

We believe Jesus Christ was born of the virgin Mary and lived a sinless life on earth.

> **He was the perfect example of how to live in relationship with God on earth.**

We believe the sacrifice of Jesus Christ on the cross is the one and final sacrifice for the sins of mankind. The only way to be forgiven of our sins (wrongs) and receive eternal life with God is acceptance in the message of Jesus Christ.

"We believe Jesus Christ was born of the virgin Mary…" Jesus Christ was immaculately conceived with no biological father, to fulfill the words of the prophet _____.

> *All this took place to fulfill what the Lord had said through the prophet: "The _____ will conceive and give birth to a son, and they will call him Immanuel" (which means "God with us").*
> (Matthew 1:22-23)

"…and lived a sinless life on earth." Jesus is fully _____ and fully _____, and while He was tempted, He did not sin.

> *For we do not have a high priest who is unable to _____ with our weaknesses, but we have one who has been tempted in every way, just as we are—yet he did not sin.*
> (Hebrews 4:15)

"He was the perfect example of how to live in relationship with God on earth." We can look to the life of Christ as an example to _____ as we seek to grow closer to God.

> But Jesus _____ withdrew to lonely places and _____.
> (Luke 5:16)

"We believe the sacrifice of Jesus Christ on the cross is the one and final sacrifice for the sins of mankind." Jesus then died on the _____ as the perfect sacrifice for our sin, and rose again on the third day.

> For by _____ he has made perfect forever those who are being made holy.
> (Hebrews 10:14)

"The only way to be _____ of our sins (wrongs) and receive eternal life with God is acceptance in the message of Jesus Christ." Because of Jesus' death and resurrection, our sins can be _____, and we have eternal life through Him and only Him.

> For God so loved the world that he gave his one and only Son, that _____ believes in him shall not perish but have eternal life.
> (John 3:16)

> Jesus answered, "I am the way and the truth and the life. No one comes to the Father _____ through me.
> (John 14:6)

> If you declare with your mouth, "Jesus is Lord," and believe in your heart that God raised him from the dead, you will be _____.
> (Romans 10:9)

EXPLORE >> WHAT WE BELIEVE

THE HOLY SPIRIT

We believe in the presence of the Holy Spirit indwelling each believer and empowering each for a Godly life. We believe in an initial experience of Holy Spirit baptism and ongoing experience that provides a Christ-follower with power for living, understanding of spiritual truth, and spiritual gifts to build up the Church.

"We believe in the presence of the Holy Spirit indwelling each believer and empowering each for a Godly life." Upon _____, we believe that the Holy Spirit is with every Christian, and empowers us for Godly living and the work of making disciples.

> *But you will receive power when the Holy Spirit comes on you; and you will be my _____ in Jerusalem, and in all Judea and Samaria, and to the ends of the earth.*
>
> (Acts 1:8)

"We believe in an initial experience of Holy Spirit baptism and ongoing experience that provides a Christ-follower with power for living, understanding of spiritual truth, and spiritual gifts to build up the Church." The indwelling of the Holy Spirit also empowers through _____ for the work of the ministry.

> *While Peter was still speaking these words, the Holy Spirit came on all who heard the message. The circumcised believers who had come with Peter were astonished that the _____ of the Holy Spirit had been poured out even on Gentiles. For they heard them speaking in tongues and praising God.*
>
> (Acts 10:44-46)

WK 2: THE STORY WE'RE IN — THE BIBLE, THE FALL, THE RETURN OF CHRIST

THE BIBLE

We believe the 66 books of the Holy Bible are the complete letters from God to mankind. We believe they were written by men as the Holy Spirit guided them. We believe the Bible is to be read and studied in order to understand: our history; man's depravity; and God's nature, character, and desire for us as we live life on earth.

"We believe the 66 books of the Holy Bible are the complete letters from God to mankind." This means that Scripture is _____ for knowing the truth that God wants communicated to us.

> *But even if we or an angel from heaven should preach a gospel _____ than the one we preached to you, let them be under God's curse! As we have already said, so now I say again: If anybody is preaching to you a gospel other than what you accepted, let them be under God's curse!*
>
> (Galatians 1:8-9)

"We believe they were written by men as the Holy Spirit guided them." This means that while the authors of the Biblical books were human, they were _____ by God in order to produce the infallible work that God wanted.

> *All Scripture is _____*
>
> (2 Timothy 3:16a)

"We believe the Bible is to be read and studied in order to understand: our history; man's depravity; and God's nature, character, and desire for us as we live life on earth." The _____ of Scripture is useful for knowing God, and living the life He wants us to live.

> *...and is useful for teaching, rebuking, correcting and training in righteousness, so that the servant of God may be _____ for every good work.*
>
> (2 Timothy 3:16b-17)

THE FALL

We believe that mankind lives in a fallen nature unworthy of God's presence due to the problem of sin, stemming from the original sin of Adam and Eve and carried through every generation since the beginning. Without a Savior, mankind is left without hope of an eternity with God.

"We believe that mankind lives in a fallen nature unworthy of God's presence due to the problem of sin,". In our natural state _____, we have no hope of eternal salvation. We are all sinful by nature.

> *for _____ have sinned and fall short of the glory of God,*
> (Romans 3:23)

> *For the wages of sin is _____, but the gift of God is eternal life in Christ Jesus our Lord.*
> (Romans 6:23)

"stemming from the original sin of Adam and Eve and carried through every generation since the beginning." Sin first entered the world through the sin of Adam and Eve, which carries _____ to us today.

> *Therefore, just as sin _____ the world through one man, and death through sin, and in this way death came to all people, because all sinned–*
> (Romans 5:12)

"Without a Savior, mankind is left without hope of an eternity with God." Our only hope for the redemption of our sin is the finished work of Christ.

> *Jesus answered, "I am the way and the truth and the life. _____ comes to the Father except through me.*
> (John 14:6)

EXPLORE WHAT WE BELIEVE

THE RETURN OF CHRIST

Also known as the Second Coming of Christ, we believe that those who have died in Christ will be united with those still alive when Christ returns. Following this will be the Millennial Reign of Christ, the Final Judgment, and finally the fulfillment of a new heaven and a new earth.

"Also known as the Second Coming of Christ, we believe that those who have died in Christ will be united with those still alive when Christ returns." At some point in the future, Christ will _____ and bring all Christians (both alive and dead) to spend eternity with Him.

> *For the Lord himself will come down from heaven, with a loud command, with the voice of the archangel and with the trumpet call of God, and the dead in Christ will rise first. After that, we who are still alive and are left will be caught up _____ with them in the clouds to meet the Lord in the air. And so we will be with the Lord forever.*
>
> (1 Thessalonians 4:16-17)

"Following this will be the Millennial Reign of Christ," In the book of Revelation we get a picture of what the return of Christ will look like. One aspect of this is a millennial period of time where Christ _____ alongside those who have given their lives for Him.

> *I saw thrones on which were seated those who had been given authority to judge. And I saw the souls of those who had been beheaded because of their testimony about Jesus and because of the word of God. They had not worshiped the beast or its image and had not received its mark on their foreheads or their hands. They came to life and reigned _____ for a thousand years.*
>
> (Revelation 20:4)

"the Final Judgment," After this millennial period, there will be a final _____ for both Satan and mankind.

> And I saw the dead, great and small, standing before the throne, and books were opened. Another book was opened, which is the book of life. The dead were judged according to what they had done as recorded in the books… Anyone whose name was not found written in the _____ was thrown into the lake of fire.
> (Revelation 20:12 & 15)

"and finally the fulfillment of a new heaven and a new earth." Our great hope in Christ is that we are redeemed by Him, and get to spend eternity in _____ relationship with God.

> Then I saw "a new _____ and a new _____," for the first heaven and the first earth had passed away, and there was no longer any sea… And I heard a loud voice from the throne saying, "Look! God's dwelling place is now among the people, and he will dwell with them. They will be his people, and God himself will be with them and be their God. 'He will wipe every tear from their eyes. There will be no more death' or mourning or crying or pain, for the old order of things has passed away."
> (Revelation 21:1 & 3-4)

EXPLORE >> 053
WHAT WE BELIEVE

WK 3: THE CHURCH AND IT'S FUNCTIONS — THE CHURCH, COMMUNION & BAPTISM, HEALING, MARRIAGE

THE CHURCH

We believe that Jesus Christ commissioned the global Church as the instrument to provide hope to the world. The Church offers this hope through the preaching of the message of Jesus Christ's sacrifice for the forgiveness of mankind. The Church also displays this hope through serving the community, helping the poor, and extending the offer of the Christian community to all.

"We believe that Jesus Christ commissioned the global Church as the instrument to provide hope to the world." When Jesus ascended into Heaven, he commanded the disciples to go and make more disciples. This is the _____ function of the Church. This Church is meant to involve all people-groups.

> *Therefore go and make disciples of _____, baptizing them in the name of the Father and of the Son and of the Holy Spirit, and teaching them to obey everything I have commanded you. And surely I am with you always, to the very end of the age.*
>
> (Matthew 28:19-20)

"The Church offers this hope through the preaching of the message of Jesus Christ's sacrifice for the forgiveness of mankind." Another key function of the Church is _____ our fellow brothers and sisters in Christ through the truth of the Gospel.

> *They devoted themselves to the apostles' _____ and to _____, to the breaking of bread and to _____.*
>
> (Acts 2:42)

"The Church also displays this hope through serving the community, helping the poor, and extending the offer of the Christian community to all." The Church's function is also to serve and provide for those in need. This is a way to _____ show the Gospel, due to how it changes how we treat others.

> *They sold property and possessions to _____ who had need.*
>
> (Acts 2:45)

COMMUNION AND BAPTISM

Also known as the Ordinances of the Church, we believe Communion and Baptism were modeled by Christ and commissioned as an ongoing remembrance of faith in Him. Communion is a corporate remembrance through bread and wine (juice) as a symbolism of the body and blood of Jesus Christ. Water baptism is a public declaration of an individual's association with Jesus Christ.

"Also known as the Ordinances of the Church, we believe Communion and Baptism were modeled by Christ and commissioned as an ongoing remembrance of faith in Him." Both Communion and Baptism are functions of the Church that we engage in to bring our minds to the _____ of the Gospel.

> Peter replied, "Repent and be _____, every one of you, in the name of Jesus Christ for the forgiveness of your sins. And you will receive the gift of the Holy Spirit.
>
> (Acts 2:28)

> For _____ you eat this bread and drink this cup, you proclaim the Lord's death until he comes.
>
> (1 Corinthians 11:26)

EXPLORE WHAT WE BELIEVE 055

"Communion is a corporate remembrance through bread and wine (juice) as a symbolism of the body and blood of Jesus Christ." When we take communion together as a church, it is a reminder of the _____ of Jesus for our sin.

> *And he took bread, gave thanks and broke it, and gave it to them, saying, "This is my body given for you; do this in _____ of me." In the same way, after the supper he took the cup, saying, "This cup is the new covenant in my blood, which is poured out for you.*
>
> (Luke 22:19-20)

"Water baptism is a public declaration of an individual's association with Jesus Christ." After salvation, the next _____ step is to be water baptized and publicly declare your faith in Christ.

> *So in Christ Jesus you are all children of God through faith, for all of you who were baptized _____ have clothed yourselves with Christ.*
>
> (Galatians 3:26-27)

HEALING

We believe that Jesus Christ's power to heal is seen in the Gospels and is available to all believers through His sacrifice. The church is to lay hands on the sick and pray the prayer of faith for an individual's divine recovery.

"We believe that Jesus Christ's power to heal is seen in the Gospels and is available to all believers through His sacrifice." While on earth Jesus _____ His disciples for healing as well, and this is extended to the Church at Christ's ascension.

> When Jesus had called the Twelve together, he gave them power and authority to drive out all demons and to _____, and he sent them out to proclaim the kingdom of God and to heal the sick.
> (Luke 9:1-2)

"The church is to lay hands on the sick and pray the prayer of faith for an individual's divine recovery." An additional function of the Church is praying for the physical _____ of people within that church.

> Is anyone among you sick? Let them call the elders of the church to pray over them and anoint them with oil in the name of the Lord. And the prayer offered in faith will make the _____; the Lord will raise them up. If they have sinned, they will be forgiven.
> (James 5:14-16)

EXPLORE WHAT WE BELIEVE » 057

MARRIAGE

Marriage is God-ordained. God's design for marriage goes back to mankind's beginning. The family, as God's means of propagating His creation, grows out of this primary human relationship. The marriage relationship encompasses the deepest unity of man and woman in its social and physical expressions. The first woman was declared to be a suitable helper for the man, the perfect complement. God intended them to share both blessings and responsibilities. Mutual esteem and self-giving love strengthen the marriage relationship. God intended this physical, emotional, intellectual, and spiritual union to be focused on one partner only. We believe that marriage is a covenant relationship between one man and woman that should last a lifetime.

"Marriage is God-ordained. God's design for marriage goes back to mankind's beginning. The family, as God's means of propagating His creation, grows out of this primary human relationship." From the very _____, marriage was the plan of God.

> Then the Lord God made a woman from the rib he had taken out of the man, and he brought her to the man.
>
> The man said,
> "This is now bone of my bones
>   and flesh of my flesh;
> she shall be called 'woman,'
>   for she was taken out of man."
>
> That is why a man leaves his father and mother and is united to his wife, and they become _____ flesh.
>
> (Genesis 2:22-24)

"The marriage relationship encompasses the deepest unity of man and woman in its social and physical expressions." The bonds of marriage go deeper than simple _____.

> For this reason a man will leave his father and mother and be united to his wife, and the two will become one flesh.' So they are no longer two, but one flesh. Therefore what God has joined together, let no one _____."
>
> (Mark 10:7-9)

"The first woman was declared to be a suitable helper for the man, the perfect complement." God created men and women to _____ each other up in their callings from God.

> The Lord God said, "It is not good for the man to be _____. I will make a helper suitable for him."
> (Genesis 2:18)

"God intended them to share both blessings and responsibilities. Mutual esteem and self-giving love strengthen the marriage relationship." Both men and women are called to make _____ for a healthy message. All Biblically healthy marriages involve shared blessings and responsibilities.

> Wives, submit yourselves to your own husbands as you do to the Lord. For the husband is the head of the wife as Christ is the head of the church, his body, of which he is the Savior. Now as the church submits to Christ, so also wives should submit to their husbands in everything. Husbands, love your wives, _____ loved the church and gave himself up for her to make her holy, cleansing her by the washing with water through the word, and to present her to himself as a radiant church, without stain or wrinkle or any other blemish, but holy and blameless. In this same way, husbands ought to love their wives as their own bodies. He who loves his wife loves himself.
> (Ephesians 5:22-28)

"God intended this physical, emotional, intellectual, and spiritual union to be focused on one partner only. We believe that marriage is a covenant relationship between one man and woman that should last a lifetime." God's _____ for marriage is for one man and one woman. We see instances of polygamy in the Old Testament; however, this is not the ideal set by God.

> "Haven't you read," he replied, "that at the beginning the Creator 'made them male and female,' and said, 'For this reason a man will leave his father and mother and be _____ to his wife, and the two will become one flesh'? So they are no longer two, but one flesh. Therefore what God has joined together, let no one separate."
> (Matthew 19:4-6)

EXPLORE | CLASS THREE

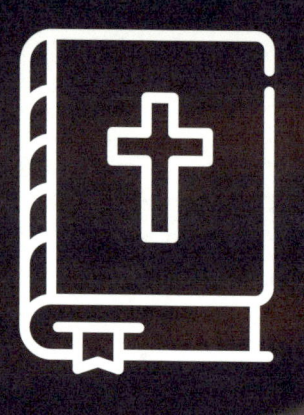

HOW TO STUDY THE BIBLE

SCAN TO SIGN UP!

OR VISIT: GROVE.CHURCH/HOW-TO-STUDY-THE-BIBLE-CLASS

ARE YOU NEW TO READING THE BIBLE? OR WOULD YOU LIKE SOME HELPFUL TIPS AND TRICKS TO GET THE MOST OUT OF YOUR BIBLE STUDY?

Then this class is for you! In the three week long How to Study the Bible class we will go over the history of how we got our Bible, how to read the different genres, and how to use the tools in the NIV Life Application Study Bible. Sign up for this class to take a next step with your Bible reading.

WEEK 1:
HOW WE GOT THE BIBLE

WEEK 2:
THE GENRES OF THE BIBLE

WEEK 3:
THE TOOLS TO STUDY THE BIBLE

EXPLORE
HOW TO STUDY THE BIBLE

WK 1: HOW WE GOT THE BIBLE

WHAT DOES IT MEAN FOR SCRIPTURE TO BE "GOD BREATHED?"

All Scripture is God-breathed and is useful for teaching, rebuking, correcting and training in righteousness, so that the servant of God may be thoroughly equipped for every good work.

We believe that the _____ of the _____ books of the Bible were _____.

Original writings: The original _____ penned by the original _____. Good translations are trustworthy, but not infallible.

66 books: The _____ of Scripture. There are other books, some helpful and some not, that we do not consider Scripture.

Inspired by God: While it is from God, it is written from a _____.

HOW DID WE GET THE OLD TESTAMENT?

The Old Testament was _____ over time. Some of this happened and is recorded in Scripture, the Law of Moses is constantly mentioned as an example.

Over time these books were copied in an extremely _____.

By the time of Christ there was _____ on what was Scripture, and Jesus does not refute any of it.

The Apocrypha was known; however, it was seen as being a rung below Scripture. While we don't believe these are the inspired Word of God, this does not make them bad. They are particularly great to understand the changes in Judaism between the time of _____ and _____.

HOW DID WE GET THE NEW TESTAMENT?

This was a much quicker process than the Old Testament, as the books are all written within about a _____ span instead of over centuries.

Contrary to what some believe, the books we have were all _____ _____ as Scripture by the Early Church. And there is no book that was widely recognized that is not included.

There was an expectation of _____. Almost every book of the New Testament was written by an Apostle (Mark, Luke, and Hebrews being the only exceptions).

- Mark was known to base his Gospel on the word of Peter, with whom he served.
- Luke interviewed eyewitnesses and Apostles to compile his Gospel.
- While the author of Hebrews is unknown, it was widely believed to be written by someone with Apostolic authority in the Early Church.

> Also contrary to what some believe, the canon was not made at the council of Nicea. It was _____ long before that, and the council was about combating heresy.

Over time these books were copied. This was a less careful method than we saw with the Old Testament. The copiers of the New Testament documents changed word order and spelling for different regions. This can sound scary, but _____ of the variants change the meaning of a verse in any way, and exactly 0 change Christian doctrine.

EXPLORE | CLASS THREE | WK 1

HOW DID WE GET OUR ENGLISH TRANSLATIONS?

Translation out of the _____ language has been a part of how God spread His word for thousands of years.

- The Septuigent (around 250 B.C.) was a Greek translation of the Old Testament, it was widely used since Greek was the lingua franca (most common language) of the time. In fact Jesus seems to quote it at times instead of the original Hebrew.
- The Vulgate (around A.D. 400) was a translation of the Old and New testament into Latin, the lingua franca of its day.
- Over time the Roman Catholic Church (the dominant church of Western Europe) came to view Latin as the only acceptable language for the Bible.

For _____ specifically we have this (simplified) timeline:

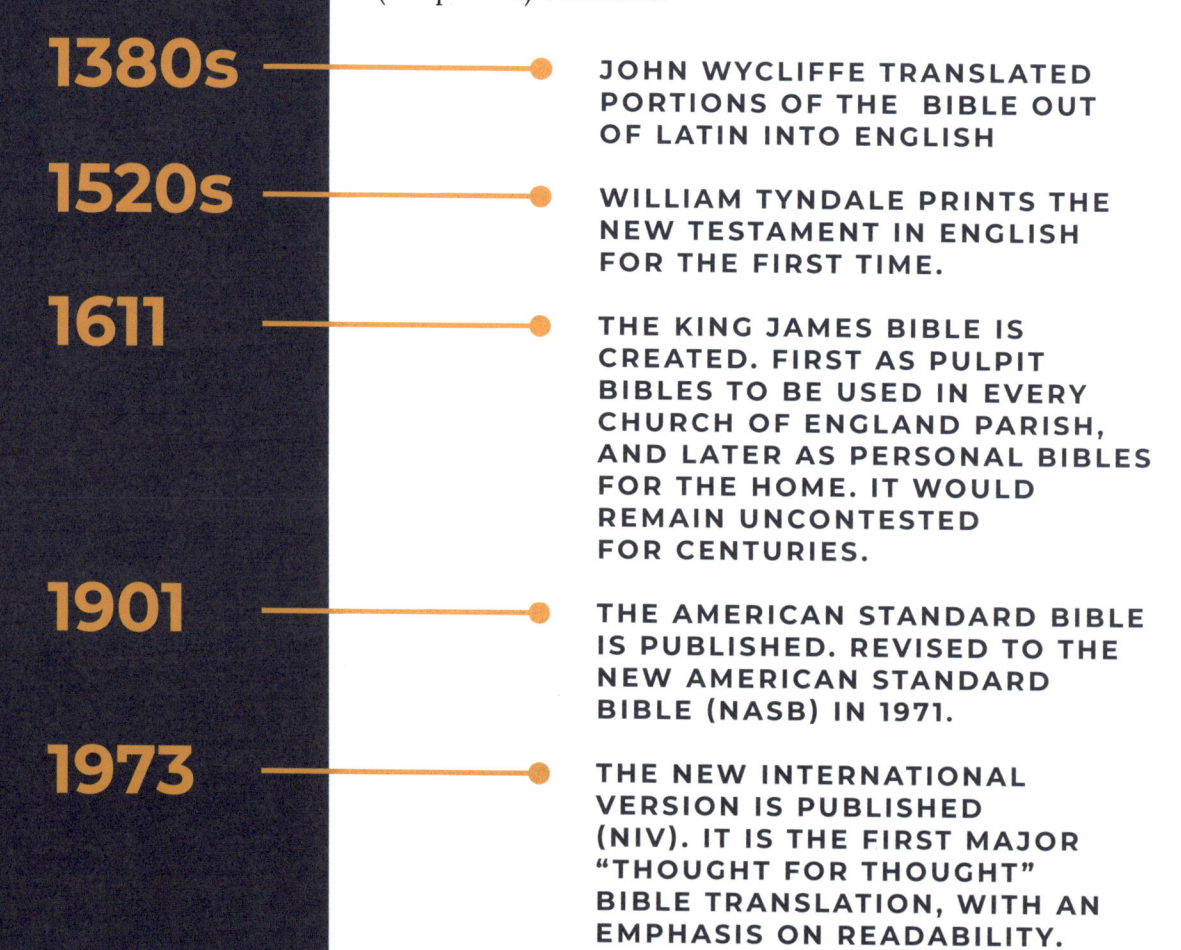

1380s — JOHN WYCLIFFE TRANSLATED PORTIONS OF THE BIBLE OUT OF LATIN INTO ENGLISH

1520s — WILLIAM TYNDALE PRINTS THE NEW TESTAMENT IN ENGLISH FOR THE FIRST TIME.

1611 — THE KING JAMES BIBLE IS CREATED. FIRST AS PULPIT BIBLES TO BE USED IN EVERY CHURCH OF ENGLAND PARISH, AND LATER AS PERSONAL BIBLES FOR THE HOME. IT WOULD REMAIN UNCONTESTED FOR CENTURIES.

1901 — THE AMERICAN STANDARD BIBLE IS PUBLISHED. REVISED TO THE NEW AMERICAN STANDARD BIBLE (NASB) IN 1971.

1973 — THE NEW INTERNATIONAL VERSION IS PUBLISHED (NIV). IT IS THE FIRST MAJOR "THOUGHT FOR THOUGHT" BIBLE TRANSLATION, WITH AN EMPHASIS ON READABILITY.

Most modern evangelical Bible translations are trustworthy. They exist on a spectrum of _____ on one end and _____ on the other. Here's some helpful examples of these:

- **Word for word:** New American Standard Bible (NASB), English Standard Bible (ESV), Legacy Standard Bible (LSB), New King James Version (NKJV). The King James Version (KJV) is in this style as well, albeit very difficult to read today.
- **Thought for thought:** Christian Standard Bible (CSV), New Living Translation (NLT), New International Version (NIV). Young children or those with learning difficulties may find the New International Reader's Version (NIrV) helpful as well.

> # Some things in Bibles are helpful, but not Scripture.

Chapters and verses. Super helpful to be able to look up something quickly, but can get us in trouble since that's not the way the books were meant to be read. Make sure not to view a new chapter or verse as a brand new _____ _____ .

Chapter headings. Again super helpful, but keep in mind that these are written by people who were not inspired by God. Sometimes you might _____ in the text because you're looking for the topic it states. If you ever want to try reading the Bible without these added features, try a _____ .

TRY IT AT HOME!

Read Mark 8:1-10 in 4 different translations listed in the examples beforehand (the Youversion Bible App is an easy way to do this) and answer the questions below:

Write down three differences you notice between the translations.

①

②

③

Which translation did you find to be the most readable?

Try reading while ignoring all the verse markers. Did that change the way you saw anything in the passage?

Our annual Carnival is one of our favorite events of the year. We open our church to thousands of people on Halloween to provide a safe place for families to play games, get to know our church, and of course get tons of candy.

We would love for you to bring your family this October 31 or, if you're able, to volunteer to be a part of the small army it takes to run this event. Scan the QR code or visit **grove.church/carnival** for more.

SCAN FOR MORE INFO!

OR VISIT: GROVE.CHURCH/CARNIVAL

CARNIVAL

WK 2: THE GENRES OF THE BIBLE

HOW TO STUDY THE OLD TESTAMENT

The story of the Road to Emmaus shows us that the whole of the Old Testament is pointing to _____.

> "²⁷ And beginning with Moses and all the Prophets, he explained to them what was said in _____ concerning himself."
>
> Luke 24:27

So there are two things that we need to keep in mind as we read through the Old Testament:

- First, how would this have been understood by those who read it for the _____?
    - This is where the notes in a study Bible will be very helpful. None of us are ancient Jews, so we need some help to understand what that would have been like. God had a message for His people at that time, and we need to know what it was.

- Second, how does this point to _____? This is for me the most fun part of reading the Old Testament. Once we understand what the original message was, we can ask ourselves how this story points to the revelation of Jesus.

NARRATIVE

This is the easiest of the genres to read, because we're all very familiar with reading it. Most books that we read, and movies or tv shows we watch, are _____.

These are stories with a beginning, middle, and end. At the base level the author is trying to convey the story of something that happened. This also includes the list of laws and descriptions of the tabernacle/temple for example. While these are really dry to read, they are pretty straightforward on interpretation.

Physical descriptions being extremely important in Hebrew Narrative. If the author is taking time to describe _____, then it's important.

POETRY

Poetry is going to make up a large portion of the Bible, particularly of the _____. The easy way to spot it is by the format of the page, when you notice that the text is not stretching all the way across the page, that's a good hint. (*Example: Job, page 787*)

Poetry is rooted in _____, so it's important to know that not everything is meant to be taken literally. A lot of it is using examples, for a deeper spiritual truth.

The big thing to know about Hebrew poetry is the idea of _____. As you read through you'll notice that almost always the line that is tabbed over further right in a pairing, is connected to the line that came before.

Some kinds of Parallelism:
- Synonymous Parallelism: the second line _____ the thought of the first. (*Example: Psalm 22, page 865*)
- Antithetical Parallelism: the second line _____ the thought of the first. (*Example: Psalm 18:26, page 861*)
- Synthetic Parallelism: the second line _____ the thought of the first. (*Example: Psalm 23, page 868*)

PROPHECY

Prophecy is a genre where people record the _____ given to prophets. God used prophets throughout history to give both encouragement and warning to His people. Not every prophet has their message or story recorded in the Bible, or in an individual book. (*Elijah and Elisha don't even have their own books!*)

Oftentimes these messages would contain predictions to show it really was from God. A common formula is a _____ prediction, and then a _____ prediction. The short term prediction was often meant to show the prophet was truly from God, and thus lead to trust in the long term prediction.

EXPLORE
HOW TO STUDY THE BIBLE

Oftentimes prophecy will have a _____ fulfillment, the Messianic prophecies are great examples. Joel 2:28-3:3 is an example of dual fulfillment. The day of the Lord where His Spirit is poured out is the day we live in now. Another aspect of that day is all the nations being judged, which has not taken place yet.

For the prophetic books, break things down to _____ or individual speeches. Each speech may have a different audience or different point.

> Keep in mind that we think of prophecy most often as prediction of the future. While that is a big part, the main point is a message from God about how His people _____ .

LETTERS

For letters, break things down by _____. Make sure you understand what each paragraph is trying to communicate.

_____ is connected to the last. When we are having a conversation, we have each thought in connection with whatever was said previously.

I think the chapter and verse system does us the most disservice in the letters of the New Testament. Keep in mind that each new "chapter" was never meant to be read that way, always ask yourself how what you are reading is _____ to what came before.

APOCALYPTIC LITERATURE

This is the most difficult genres of the Bible to understand, primarily because it is prophecy that has not _____.

My advice for these is to let your imagination run, but also keep it on a leash. This is a bit of a contradiction; I suppose what I mean is to not be too dogmatic with how we interpret the intentionally confusing sections in this genre. Much like the Pharisees discovered with the Messianic prophecies, we probably aren't going to get it right.

This is a pretty small genre, the only book that is majority apocalyptic is _____, however there are also long passages in Daniel.

Apocalyptic literature is concerned with the end, which means the _____ _____ and creation of the New Heaven and New Earth.

TRY IT AT HOME!

Below are some sample passages from each genre. Read each and answer the questions that follow.

NARRATIVE - READ JUDGES 3:12-30
What was the physical characteristic of Ehud mentioned that made a difference in the story?

POETRY - READ PSALM 117
What kind of parallelism(s) is being used in this passage?

PROPHECY - READ ISAIAH 7:10-17
Can you think of how this prophecy was fulfilled in two ways?

LETTERS - READ 3 JOHN
In one sentence each, describe the idea of each paragraph.

APOCALYPTIC LITERATURE - READ REVELATION 21:1-8
How does this description of the return of Christ make you feel?

WK 3: HOW TO USE A STUDY BIBLE

> Remember that all the tools we're talking about today are _____, but not the perfect Word of God. They don't hold the same _____ as Scripture.

CROSS REFERENCES

Signified by a lowercase _____ letter. These show other places in the Bible where that same theme may be explored, or where the text may be _____.
- Example: Matthew 27:46 (page 1653) shows a connection of Jesus' words in Matthew with Psalm 22.

FOOTNOTES

Signified by a lowercase _____ letter. Give helpful notes on possible different ways to translate a word or thought or show a textual variant, bring uncertain Hebrew words into modern English, among _____.
- Matthew 27:46 (page 1653) is an example of a textual variant.
- Exodus 38:21-31 (page 149) is an example of bringing an ancient word into modern English. Usually these are measurements or diseases.

TIMELINE

A great resource for seeing where events take place within other _____. Biblical events are listed on the top, with other events listed below.
- Found on page A18

NOTES

Found under the red line on every page, these are helpful _____ on the verses above. Sometimes providing application, or helpful context on more difficult to understand verses.

Use these as a great way to help you understand what is happening in a verse that maybe is difficult to understand. For controversial verses, I always recommend getting the opinions of _____ commentators.

This Bible also contains notes on how to _____ a verse to your life today.

BOOK INTRODUCTIONS

- Example Joshua, page 303

Vital Statistics - This gives some _____ of and what is coming up in a book.

Overview - A short _____ that introduces the book.

Timeline - Helps you see _____ in the Biblical story this book takes place. (Super helpful with the prophets).

Blueprint - Gives you a nice _____ of the book. (I find these most helpful with the wisdom literature and the prophets).

Megathemes - Gives an overview of some of the themes that are _____ within the book.

Map - Helps you see _____ the events of the book take place, and where key locations are.

EXPLORE >> 077
HOW TO STUDY THE BIBLE

HARMONIES

- Found on pages 556 & 1853

Super helpful to _____ the two great stories where we see it from multiple perspectives: the reigns of the kings of Israel, and the ministry of Jesus. A harmony helps blend the accounts together into one timeline. These are also built into headings in the Gospels.

These also help show what the different authors are trying to _____ in their stories. Why did they choose to include or omit information?

PERSONALITY PROFILES

Short biographies of major _____ as they are introduced.
- Example Joshua 3, page 309

MAPS

In the back, these help bring Biblical _____ to life.

CHARTS & DIAGRAMS

Found throughout the text, they give helpful _____ of different ideas.
- Example: page 302 shows different names for God.

ARTICLES

Longer articles about _____ topics found throughout the Bible.
- Example: The Time Between the Testaments on page 1571.

INDEX

The index in this Bible shows you every chart, map, and personality profile in the Bible. If you want to _____ about a topic, look it up in the index, and then look up the corresponding resource.
- Master Index - Page 2273
- Index to Charts - Page 2377
- Index to Maps - Page 2381
- Index to Personality Profiles - Page 2383

DICTIONARY/CONCORDANCE

Here you can look up words and see a quick _____, and some places where it is used in the Bible. Note that this is not an exhaustive concordance, but hits most of the words people would be looking for.
- Found on page 2385

EXPLORE
HOW TO STUDY THE BIBLE

TRY IT AT HOME!

We won't be meeting to go over this, so it's on the honor system! Choose a book of the Bible that you have read before. Read the book introduction. List five things that you learned from that introduction that you didn't know before.

①

②

③

④

⑤

THE CODE

SERIOUS

We are serious about the saving work of Jesus Christ.

We know the methods will change but the message never will.

EXPLORE THE CODE 083

HOW TO USE THE
YOUVERSION BIBLE APP

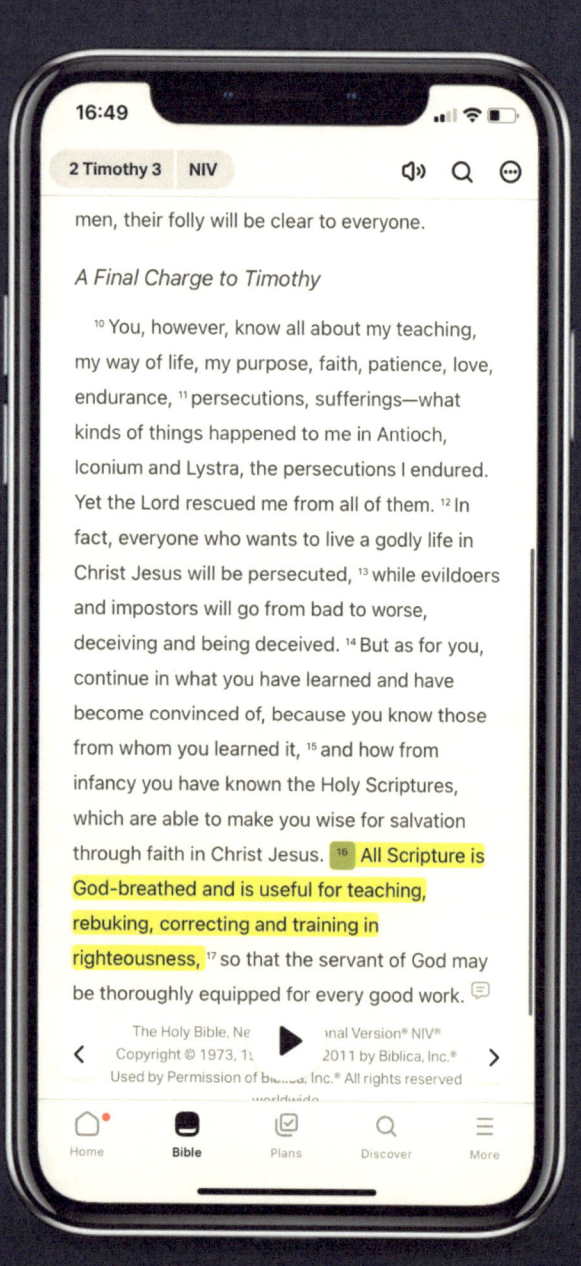

The Youversion Bible App is a wonderful tool for helping you with Bible reading. Just imagine how blessed all the Christians of the past would feel to have dozens of Bible translations and articles in the palm of their hands. For most of Christian history the idea of owning your own copy of the Bible was a pipe dream, and now it's 100% free. While you can't replace the feel of a physical Bible that you can mark up yourself, the tools found on this smartphone app can still help you even if you're dedicated to reading a physical Bible. In this short article, we'll go over some of the tools available on the app!

HOME: When you download the app and get it all set up you'll notice that the first page you're on is the home page. On this page you'll find reading plans that you are subscribed to, which is very helpful for keeping up with your reading. The other big category is called "Community". This allows you to follow along with other people's activity on the app, and add friends. Remember, Bible study is meant to be done in a community where we can all encourage one another.

BIBLE: The next section is where the Bible portion of the Bible app comes in. When you click here you can access any portion of the Bible in almost every English translation. This is great for comparing what different trusted translations say with any given verse (for examples of trusted translations see the "Which Bible is Best For You" article in this book). There is also a great feature where the app will read the Bible to you. Even if you are on the go and driving around, you can still hear Biblical truth. You can also highlight different verses to come back to later.

PLANS: The next section is where you can find and start different Bible reading plans. These plans are incredibly diverse. Some of them are "Bible in a year" plans, which as the name suggests help you read through the whole Bible in a year. Other plans take you through a specific book of the Bible. While other plans can go over different topics as you work through studies of what the Bible has to say on that subject. There really is an embarrassment of riches when it comes to reading plans to help you keep your Bible reading fresh.

DISCOVER: In this section of the app you can search for all sorts of different things. This can be a topic to see where it comes up in the Bible or plans related to that topic. You can search for a church to set as your home church (which if you're reading this is probably the Grove Church). You can also search through short teaching clips from different Christians that Youversion is highlighting.

MORE: The final section is the "More" section, which of course has a bunch of different options. We don't have space to go over everything, but here are a couple highlights. First there is a verse of the day that gives you a different Bible verse to think upon everyday. There is a section for guided prayer that helps you walk through a prayer time with Scripture to meditate on. You can also see all of the verses that you've highlighted in one specific section.

Hopefully this is helpful for you if you choose to utilize the Youversion Bible app. Make sure to check it out for yourself and explore!

WHICH BIBLE IS BEST FOR YOU?

TRANSLATIONS

This is a great question, and there is no one right answer for everyone. The first step is to make sure that you have a translation that is reliable. At the Grove Church, we recommend modern Evangelical committee translations. Which means they are done by multiple believers in Christ.

These translations are on a spectrum. On the one side, you have translations that prioritize readability. This means that in areas where the language is difficult to understand, the translators engage in extra interpretation to help the meaning come through. These can also be called "thought for thought" translations. Examples of these would be the New International Version (NIV) and the New Living Translation (NLT).

On the other side, you have translations that prioritize accuracy to the original words. This means that you are getting as close as possible to the original text, however it is often more difficult to read. Examples of these would be the English Standard Version (ESV), New King James Bible (NKJV), New American Standard Bible (NASB). A translation that exists in between the two sides is the Christian Standard Bible (CSV).

We recommend that everyone read multiple trusted translations in their lives. No one translation is perfect, so reading multiple translations will help you get the most understanding out of God's word. For new Christians, we think it's helpful to start with a more readable translation like the NIV or NLT.

KIND OF BIBLE

There are many different types of Bibles that can help you in your study as well, far too many to go over in this short article. For now let's focus on two types:

First, study Bibles. These are Bibles that come with all sorts of tools built into the text itself. They will have helpful commentary on each verse to help when going through a difficult passage, references and footnotes to help see how other parts of the Bible connect, and so much more.

Second, readers Bibles. These are almost the polar opposite of study Bibles. Where the study Bible is all about giving you tools to help you understand, readers Bibles are all about giving you the experience of reading the original text as much as possible.

The eliminate verse numbers, title headings, and oftentimes chapter numbers as well. The reason is to give you as smooth an experience of reading as possible, without being distracted by the (still helpful) tools that were added into our Bibles later. This could be a great Bible to try out once you feel like you have a handle on the overall themes of Scripture.

With all of this in mind, the Bible that we recommend for new believers and seasoned believers alike is the NIV Life Application Study Bible. It is a readable translation, and has a ton of helpful tools for the reader. In our How to Study the Bible class you can learn about studying the Bible in general andusing the NIV Life Application Study Bible in particular.

NEXT STEPS

JOIN A BIBLE READING PLAN

You may be asking what the importance of consistent Bible reading is. After all, when you go to church you are hearing the Bible weekly. But this attitude reveals a misunderstanding of what we have when we hold our Bibles.

> God has chosen to directly communicate with all Humanity, how on earth could we not want to know everything we can about it?

How often do we wish that God would speak to us, when over on our shelf we have 66 books inspired by God that communicate His truth to us every day? Staying in God's Word helps us to combat believing lies about who He is, and how we should live.

A Bible reading plan is a great way to stay consistent with your reading. First, there is a level of accountability when you are reading something with other people from the church. Maybe as a Life Group you can all jump in and talk about what you've been reading. Plus let's be honest, there's something helpful about checking off a box every day and seeing that progress bar grow. Consider joining a Bible reading plan to help with your consistent habit of Bible reading.

We have a reading plan to go through the whole Bible, and a plan to go through the Gospel of John to get your feet wet if you're new to this!

SCAN ME!

OR VISIT: GROVE.CHURCH/READINGPLAN

WHAT TYPE OF READING PLAN ARE YOU MOST INTERESTED IN STARTING? WHAT OTHER HABITS COULD YOU START THAT WOULD HELP YOU READ MORE CONSISTENTLY?

EXPLORE
BIBLE READING PLAN

NEXT STEPS

CREATE A WORSHIP PLAYLIST

Consider making a playlist with Biblically sound Christian music. These can be songs that we sing together on Sundays, or other music that turns your heart toward the Lord. Throughout the day, whether while driving, walking, or in a moment of reflection, listening to a personal playlist of Christian music can help set your heart right for the day. As a help we've included a playlist of the songs that we sing together as a church.

SCAN ME!

OR VISIT: QRCO.DE/WORSHIP-PLAYLIST

LIST SOME OF YOUR FAVORITE WORSHIP SONGS AND WHY THEY ARE IMPORTANT TO YOU:

WHAT IS "WORSHIP"?

"Worship" is a word we hear thrown around a lot in Christian circles, and honestly the way we use it can be confusing! To make things worse, the way scripture uses the word "worship" is different from how we tend to use it in our modern church context. This word can be a source of confusion for new (or seasoned) believers, so let's clear some things up.

The English word "worship" comes from an Old English word meaning "worthiness" or "worth-ship". The word was used to describe the act of assigning worth to something through thought or action. In modern English we tend to use the term more generally to describe an act of affection or reverence, typically in a religious context. Over time we began using the term to describe the music portion of the church service. Music is a wonderful way for us to express affection, reverence, thankfulness, and praise to the Lord, so the usage stuck!

But there's a problem: Scripture doesn't use the word "worship" this way. The word in the New Testament that is commonly translated in our English Bibles as "worship" has a meaning much closer to "service", in the way that you would serve a king or master, not church music. Understanding this discrepancy between our common usage and the way the writers of scripture use the term is critical to understanding some very important passages in the New Testament. The Apostle Paul, when writing to the church in Rome, gives us one of the most helpful passages in all of the New Testament for understanding what it means to worship:

> *Therefore, I urge you, brothers and sisters, in view of God's mercy, to offer your bodies as a living sacrifice, holy and pleasing to God—this is your true and proper worship.*
> (Romans 12:1)

Paul is teaching us what it truly means to worship the Lord. True worship is a response to the mercy that God has shown us through his Son Jesus. Paul calls us to present our bodies as a "living sacrifice", which means to offer our whole selves to the Lord: our thoughts, feelings, abilities, passions, ambition, focus and affection... the entirety of our lives!

We're told by Paul to present ourselves as "holy and acceptable" to God. The word "holy" here means set-apart or unique. Our relationship with God is meant to be set-apart high above any other relationship we have. Our reverence and affection towards Him should be unmatched. Our trust in Him should be unique. There is no one like the Lord, and our life of service to Him should reflect His holiness.

Notice that Paul says that our worship should be "acceptable to God". This means that I don't worship God however I want, just offering Him things that are convenient. God wants me to worship him in a way that is obedient. This means searching God's word to guide us towards proper service to God. This means learning to listen and yield to the Spirit of God moving and speaking in our lives.

Biblical worship isn't limited to songs we sing together on Sunday morning, even though that is one way to worship the Lord. Biblical worship is a life lived in obedient service to God, seeking to honor and bless him with everything that we do!

SECTION TWO
ENGAGE »

ENGAGE | CLASS ONE

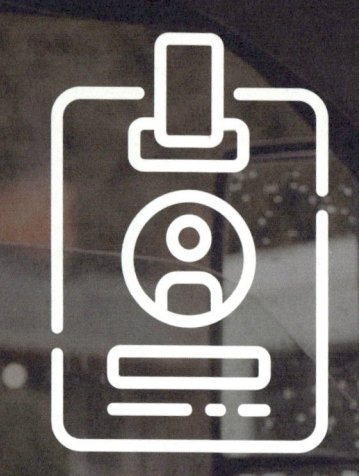

ENGAGE: USING WHO YOU ARE FOR GOD'S MISSION

SCAN TO SIGN UP!

OR VISIT: GROVE.CHURCH/EXPLORE-ENGAGE-LEAD-NIGHTS

THIS IS THE SECOND PHASE IN YOUR PATH TO CHRISTIAN MATURITY.

If the Explore class was all about who we are as a church, the Engage class is all about who you are, and how you can use your gifts for the Kingdom of God. In other words, if the Grove Church is your church, take this class to help see how you can engage with our mission.

The Engage class is part of our quarterly Explore → Engage → Lead nights. When you attend you will have dinner with everyone attending that event, and then break off for the Engage class.

WE HOPE YOU TAKE THIS NEXT STEP!

WHO YOU ARE IN CHRIST

The "Imago Dei" which means, the image of God. We are all _____ in the image of God, and because of this, worthy of dignity.

> Then God said, "Let us make mankind in our image, in our likeness, so that they may rule over the fish in the sea and the birds in the sky, over the livestock and all the wild animals, and over all the creatures that move along the ground."
>
> So God created mankind in _____ image,
>   in the image of God he created them;
>   male and female he created them.
>
> (Genesis 1:26-27)

> **The main thing that _____ us is that we are loved by God, and saved by the work of Christ.**

BEING ON MISSION

If our last class, "Explore", was about who we are as a church; "Engage" is in part about helping you figure out _____, and how you are called to use your gifts and talents to further the mission of God through the Church.

At the Grove, we believe that the spiritual gifts of the _____ are active today, and and as believers we can earnestly pray for and expect to operate in some of these gifts. As the "capital c" Church we all have our part to play in God's mission for the world, and we also have our parts to play within our own "lowercase c" church.

First, these parts can be natural talents that we possess. Think about what you are _____, and how you can use that to further the Gospel.

We won't be able to dive into this in depth, but we do offer a _____ class that we would love for you to take. Here are the Biblical Spiritual gifts, which we take from lists in Romans and 1 Corinthians 12 respectively.

ENGAGE | CLASS ONE

PROPHECY
Declaring the truth of God, specifically through divine revelation that is _____ by Scripture.

SERVING
Performing acts of _____ for others, demonstrating God's love through action.

TEACHING
Presenting the truth of Scripture and the Gospel in a way that people are able to _____.

ENCOURAGING
_____ fellow believers in their walk with God. Encouraging believers as they grow into Christian maturity.

GIVING
Joyfully giving time and money for the work of the _____.

LEADERSHIP
_____ over and leading in the context of a local church body (not just the lead pastor).

MERCY
Showing _____ and encouraging those who are suffering and going through trials.

WORDS OF WISDOM
Providing practical _____ of the wisdom of God as revealed in Scripture to our lives.

WORDS OF KNOWLEDGE
Receiving words from the Lord that reveal _____ in situations.

FAITH
Encouraging others through your _____ belief in God and His Word.

HEALING
God working through you to accomplish the _____ _____ of others.

MIRACULOUS POWERS
God working through you to perform _____ of the miraculous that glorify God.

DISCERNMENT
A supernatural ability to _____ true doctrine from false, or true and false teachers

SPEAKING IN TONGUES
The ability to speak in a _____ that you yourself do not know in order to proclaim the Gospel. In addition, the ability to speak in a language incomprehensible to man for personal edification.

INTERPRETATION OF TONGUES
The supernatural ability to _____ a language you yourself do not know. In addition, the supernatural ability to interpret a language incomprehensible to man.

ENGAGE >> 099
USING WHO YOU ARE FOR GOD'S MISSION

ENGAGE | CLASS ONE

> Keep in mind that even if you don't have a specific gift, that doesn't mean that you are never expected to still exercise that gift at times.

For instance not all have the spiritual gift of teaching, but all Christians should be able to communicate what they believe.

And a final word of caution that is incredibly important for us to remember. After Paul lists the gifts in 1 Corinthians, he says this:

> *Are all apostles? Are all prophets? Are all teachers? Do all work miracles? Do all possess gifts of healing? Do all speak with tongues? Do all interpret? But earnestly desire the higher gifts. And I will show you a still more excellent way. If I speak in the tongues of men and of angels, but have not _____, I am a noisy gong or a clanging cymbal. And if I have prophetic powers, and understand all mysteries and all knowledge, and if I have all faith, so as to remove mountains, but have not love, I am nothing. If I give away all I have, and if I deliver up my body to be burned, but have not love, I gain _____.*
>
> (1 Corinthians 12:27-13:3)

GROWING IN CHRISTIAN MATURITY

Another thing that we want to accomplish in this class is lay out what we would call the marks of a _____ Christian. This is not an exhaustive list by any means, but some helpful markers that we have. As you grow in your relationship with God here at the Grove, these are some of the goal posts we are looking for:

DISPLAY OF THE FRUIT OF THE SPIRIT

We get these from the letter of Paul to the Galatian church. In this passage he lists off two groups, one called the works of the flesh, and the other called the fruit of the Spirit.

> *Now the works of the flesh are evident: sexual immorality, impurity, sensuality, idolatry, sorcery, enmity, strife, jealousy, fits of anger, rivalries, dissensions, divisions, envy, drunkenness, orgies, and things like these. I warn you, as I warned you before, that those who do such things will not inherit the kingdom of God. But the _____ of the Spirit is* **love, joy, peace, patience, kindness, goodness, faithfulness, gentleness, self-control**; *against such things there is no law. And those who belong to _____ have crucified the flesh with its passions and desires.*
> (Galatians 5:19-24)

VIBRANT, CONSISTENT, SPIRITUAL DISCIPLINES

BIBLE READING AND STUDY

Taking consistent time to not only read God's Word, but to work to _____ what it means.

> *All Scripture is God-breathed and is useful for teaching, rebuking, correcting and training in righteousness, so that the servant of God may be thoroughly _____ for every good work.*
> (2 Timothy 3:16)

ENGAGE 101
USING WHO YOU ARE FOR GOD'S MISSION

PRAYER AND MEDITATION

Taking consistent time to have a _____ with God through prayer, and meditating on His Word.

> *Rejoice always, pray _____, give thanks in all circumstances; for this is God's will for you in Christ Jesus.*
> (1 Thessalonians 5:16-18)

FASTING

Taking time to practice the discipline of depriving yourself of something (traditionally food) for a short period to _____ on your relationship with God.

> *"_____, do not look somber as the hypocrites do, for they disfigure their faces to show others they are fasting. Truly I tell you, they have received their reward in full. But when you fast, put oil on your head and wash your face, so that it will not be obvious to others that you are fasting, but only to your Father, who is unseen; and your Father, who sees what is done in secret, will reward you.*
> (Matthew 6:16-18)

HABIT OF CONSUMING CHRIST-CENTERED CONTENT

Filing your life with intentional content that _____ your heart to the Lord. This could be music, books, podcasts, any number of things.

> *Finally, brothers and sisters, whatever is true, whatever is noble, whatever is right, whatever is pure, whatever is lovely, whatever is admirable—if anything is excellent or praiseworthy— _____ such things.*
> (Philippians 4:8)

CONSISTENT SERVING
(BOTH CHURCH BODY AND OTHERS)

Actively involved in the _____. As a church we are responsible for pushing the mission of God forward here on Earth.

> *Now you are the _____, and each one of you is a part of it. And God has placed in the church first of all apostles, second prophets, third teachers, then miracles, then gifts of healing, of helping, of guidance, and of different kinds of tongues. Are all apostles? Are all prophets? Are all teachers? Do all work miracles? Do all have gifts of healing? Do all speak in tongues? Do all interpret? Now eagerly desire the greater gifts.*
> (1 Corinthians 12:27-31)

Actively finding ways to _____ serve others.

> **This means that our serving is not just for those within our church, but for whoever we can.**

In fact this is a tangible way to show God's love to others.

> "Then the righteous will answer him, 'Lord, when did we see you hungry and feed you, or thirsty and give you something to drink? When did we see you a stranger and invite you in, or needing clothes and clothe you? When did we see you sick or in prison and go to visit you?'
>
> "The King will reply, 'Truly I tell you, whatever you did for one of _____ brothers and sisters of mine, you did for _____.'
> (Matthew 25:37-40)

GENEROSITY

Giving for the _____ of the local church. This is consistent giving toward both the workers, programs, and physical building of the church. It allows us to do what we do.

> *The elders who direct the affairs of the church well are worthy of double honor, especially those whose work is preaching and teaching. For _____, "Do not muzzle an ox while it is treading out the grain," and "The worker deserves his wages."*
> (1 Timothy 5:17-18)

Giving above and beyond to those in need. This is a way where your own giving can be _____ and _____ for you. Find people in your life who could benefit from your generosity. Are there Christ-centered charities you would love to support? How about a missionary working with a people group you are passionate about?

> *"Do not store up for yourselves treasures on earth, where moths and vermin destroy, and where thieves break in and steal. But store up for yourselves treasures in heaven, where moths and vermin do not destroy, and where thieves do not break in and steal. For where your _____ is, there your _____ will be also.*
> (Matthew 6:19-21)

LIVING IN COMMUNITY

Making an effort to cultivate authentic _____ friendships and help others feel connected to the church.

> *He died for us so that, whether we are awake or asleep, we may live _____ with him. Therefore encourage one another and build each other up, just as in fact you are doing.*
>
> (1 Thessalonians 5:10-11)

LEADING AND INFLUENCING OTHERS

Helping others in the church _____ in their relationships with Christ.

> *He began to speak boldly in the synagogue. When Priscilla and Aquila heard him, they invited him to their home and _____ to him the way of God more adequately.*
>
> (Acts 18:26)

YOUR NEXT STEPS

The next class in your Path to Christian Maturity is the Lead Class, which will be available in the next three to six months. In the meantime we would highly recommend taking at least _____ steps located in section 1 of your Next Steps Book.

NEXT STEPS

LIVING GENEROUSLY

In our Engage class we talked about the importance of serving God with our money, and how our giving should be for both the upkeep of our church and the global work of the Gospel.

FOR THIS STEP, BEGIN GIVING IN THESE AREAS:

For **giving for the church** this can be through consistent giving during a gathering, or even setting up recurring giving on the website.

SCAN ME!

OR VISIT: QRCO.DE/PUSH-PAY-GIVE

For **giving beyond the church** consider finding a missionary or Christian charity that speaks to your heart and take the step to give to their mission.

SCAN ME!

OR VISIT: GROVE.CHURCH/MISSIONS

HAVE YOU EVER CONSIDERED YOUR MONEY NOT BEING "YOURS", BUT GOD'S YOU GET TO STEWARD HERE ON EARTH? BEYOND THE CHURCH, WHAT OTHER CAUSES WOULD YOU PRAYERFULLY CONSIDER GIVING TO?

THE CODE

GENEROUS

We will lead the way with **irrational** generosity.

We believe it is more blessed to **give** than to receive.

NEXT STEPS

PRAYER AND FASTING

In addition to prayer, one discipline that we see presented throughout Scripture is fasting. Fasting is simply defined as abstaining from food for a period of time. In the Old Covenant the first fast was for the Day of Atonement, where the High Priest would offer a sacrifice for all of the people. Moving forward in the Old Testament we see multiple Bible characters engage in fasting during different seasons. Famously, Jesus fasts for 40 days in the wilderness before beginning His ministry.

We believe at the Grove that it is healthy to establish a habit of fasting. There is no Biblical mandate on how often this is, so that is up for each person to decide. When we see fasting in the Bible, it is always the full abstention from food. This could be skipping one meal, a 24 hour period, or multiple days. We would caution you to make sure that while fasting you are doing so in a healthy manner that does not endanger you.

Another kind of fasting that is not found in the Bible, but can still be healthy is to give up certain things other than food, or different types of food. This can help lead to a longer period of fasting. For instance the "Daniel fast" is a type of fast where you only eat fruits and vegetables. Some people fast technology such as social media for a period of time. Think about what God may be leading you to do!

A couple final thoughts. First, make sure to set aside time for extended prayer during your fast. As you fast, you want to make this a time of pursuing authentic relationship with the Lord, not simply not eating. The second is an important reminder that Jesus gives us in Matthew 6:16-18:

> "When you fast, do not look somber as the hypocrites do, for they disfigure their faces to show others they are fasting. Truly I tell you, they have received their reward in full. But when you fast, put oil on your head and wash your face, so that it will not be obvious to others that you are fasting, but only to your Father, who is unseen; and your Father, who sees what is done in secret, will reward you."

The principle of this passage is not that we should pour oil over our heads when we fast, but rather that we should not draw attention to ourselves.

> **Fasting is meant to be a moment between us as individuals and God, not something we do to impress others.**

AS YOU TAKE THIS STEP, THINK ABOUT HOW YOU PLAN ON FASTING, AND RECORD YOUR EXPERIENCE BELOW WHEN YOU HAVE FINISHED.

THE CODE
SACRIFICE

We give up things we love for things we love even more.

The church does not exist for us. We are the church and we exist for the world.

NEXT STEPS

FIND YOUR TEAM

One of the absolute best ways to get plugged into the church is by joining one of the serve teams. As we talked about in the Engage class, we believe a mark of Christian maturity is serving others, both through the local church and on your own.

When you join a team it gives you the opportunities to use your gifts to help the local church, as well as get to know people who you may have never met otherwise. No matter where you are at, there is a serve team for you!

WHAT TEAM DID YOU DECIDE TO JOIN?

SCAN ME!

OR VISIT: GROVE.CHURCH/FIND-YOUR-TEAM

GROVE KIDS	 WORSHIP TEAM	 PRODUCTION TEAM
 CAFE TEAM	 MEDIA TEAM	 KITCHEN TEAM
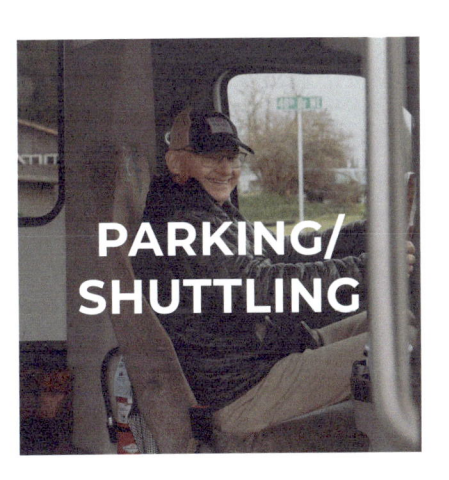 PARKING/ SHUTTLING	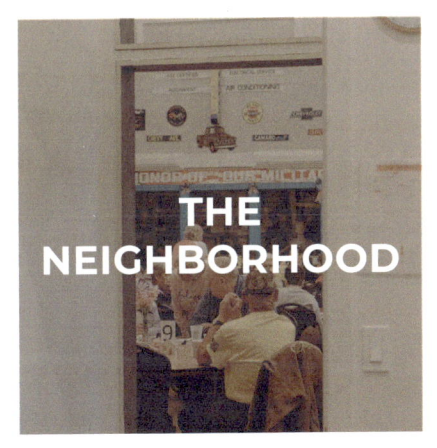 THE NEIGHBORHOOD	 AND MORE!

ENGAGE
FIND YOUR TEAM
115

THE CODE
FUN

We will laugh hard, loud, and often.

Nothing is more fun than serving God with people you love.

ENGAGE | CLASS TWO

HOW YOU'RE WIRED

SCAN TO SIGN UP!
OR VISIT: GROVE.CHURCH/HOW-YOURE-WIRED

UNDERSTANDING WHO YOU ARE AND HOW GOD HAS WIRED YOU IS ESSENTIAL TO LIVING OUT GOD'S CALL ON YOUR LIFE.

There are several facets that merge together to help you accomplish the work God has created for you in advance to do.

In this class, we will explore, in some detail, these major facets: Spiritual Gifts, Passions, Abilities, Talents and Experiences. Learning more about how you are wired should lead to greater confidence in how God created you, and greater clarity in knowing what you can do to see His kingdom work unfold.

THE CHURCH BODY

We've talked about identity in this journey, that we are created in God's image, set apart and chosen for kingdom work. The conversation continues to discuss how you and I are wired to _____ the work God has put in place for us before we were created.

- Genesis 1 - God's image
- 1 Peter - Royal Priesthood
- Ephesians 2 - Masterpiece
- John 1:12-13 - Children of God

Knowing who you are is the _____ that leads to knowing how you are wired. God creates us on purpose with purpose.

> *Just as a body, though one, has many parts, but all its many parts form _____, so it is with Christ.*
>
> (1 Corinthians 12:12)

KNOWING HOW ARE YOU WIRED

This is multifaceted and dynamic as we are all created uniquely and for a lifelong journey, but there are some _____ truths to help us become all that God intended us to be.

THE TRUTH: YOU ARE A STEWARD. (1 PETER 4:10)

A steward is defined as one who is entrusted to _____ the property of another. We have been given gifts, talents, and abilities that we are called to steward or manage - yet they are not ours. We have been given these things to use how God intended them to be used (1 Corinthians 12:7; 14:12; Ephesians 2:12-13).

SO HOW AM I WIRED?

One word of advice before we begin. We must cover all this work in _____, asking the Holy Spirit to grant us wisdom and understanding, boldness and courage to follow His leading, and discernment to know how we are wired.

The following is a brief overview of the book, S.H.A.P.E. by Eric Rees and Rick Warren.

WHY SPIRITUAL GIFTS?

God gives us gifts for _____ the Gospel with others...

> *But you will receive power when the Holy Spirit comes on you; and you will be my witnesses in Jerusalem, and in all Judea and Samaria, and to the ends of the earth.*
>
> (Acts 1:8)

...and for _____ the body of Christ. (1 Corinthians 12-14; Romans 12).

> *Now to each one the manifestation of the Spirit is given for the common good. To one there is given through the Spirit a message of wisdom, to another a message of knowledge by means of the same Spirit, to another faith by the same Spirit, to another gifts of healing by that one Spirit, to another miraculous powers, to another prophecy, to another distinguishing between spirits, to another speaking in different kinds of tongues, and to still another the interpretation of tongues. All these are the work of one and the same Spirit, and he distributes them to each one, just as he determines.*
>
> (1 Corinthians 12:7-11)

ENGAGE | CLASS TWO

As Christians, we are commanded to fulfill the _____ . We are not called to sit and wait for the time when Christ returns, we are empowered to fulfill the great commissions now.

> Then Jesus came to them and said, "All authority in heaven and on earth has been given to me. Therefore go and make disciples of all nations, baptizing them in the name of the Father and of the Son and of the Holy Spirit, and teaching them to obey everything I have commanded you. And surely I am _____ always, to the very end of the age.
>
> (Matthew 28:18-20)

WHAT SPIRITUAL GIFTS DO I HAVE?

Scan the QR code below for a link to a spiritual gifts test, or visit the link. When you have a chance take the test and take a look at the results.

SCAN ME!

OR VISIT: WWW.FREESHAPETEST.COM

WHAT ARE YOUR TOP 3 SPIRITUAL GIFTS?

HOW DO I STEWARD THESE SPIRITUAL GIFTS?

Knowing how the Holy Spirit has gifted us is only the beginning. We must learn to _____ them well.

- Study Scripture where these gifts are mentioned.
- Ask the Holy Spirit to teach you.
- Pay attention to not just what, but how they are talked about and used throughout Scripture.
- Look for opportunities to step out in faith and operate in your gifts. Sometimes it will be easy and obvious, other times it will require a bold step.

HEART / PASSION

What motivates you, compels you to action?

> "Refers to empathy, attraction, or 'draw' towards a group of people, field of expertise, or a particular type of service."
>
> (page 44 of S.H.A.P.E.)

We all have natural _____ and heartbeats that capture our attention and stir us up. The quest of discovering this will be, when inspired by the Holy Spirit, life giving and exciting. Pay attention to what those passions are, and ask prayerfully for the Holy Spirit to _____ you in the following questions.

5 PRINCIPLES TO LEARN ABOUT YOUR HEARTBEAT:

① KNOW WHAT DRIVES YOU.

- What do my dreams and desires drift toward?
- What do I really want to do for God?
- What motivates me to take action?
- What do I crave?

② KNOW WHO YOU CARE ABOUT.

- Who do I feel I can most profoundly influence for God?
- What age range do I feel led to minister too?
- What affinity group do I feel led to serve?
- How could I impact them in a way that maximizes my gifts?

③ KNOW THE NEEDS YOU WILL MEET.
Spiritual, physical, relational, emotional, educational, vocational.

- What are the top two needs I love meeting?
- Why do I love meeting these needs?
- What lessons have I learned that I could pass on to others?

④ KNOW THE CAUSE YOU WILL HELP CONQUER.

- What cause or issue makes my heart race?
- Where could I make the greatest impact for God?
- If time wasn't an issue, to what cause would I donate myself?

⑤ KNOW YOUR ULTIMATE DREAM FOR GOD'S KINGDOM.

- What pursuit would release the passion in my life for God?
- What God-centered dreams can I identify that have been buried by life?
- What would I attempt for God with the rest of my life?

YOUR ABILITIES

Natural talents and skills that you ------------------.

> *"Show me a person who doesn't know his talents or hasn't developed them for service to others, and I will show you a person who has little sense of purpose, meaning, motivation and value."*
>
> (Tom Patterson)

WHAT DO YOU LOVE DOING?

WHAT DO YOU NATURALLY EXCEL AT?

EXAMPLES: LOVE TO INSPIRE OTHERS, WORK WITH YOUR HANDS, MUSICALLY TALENTED, TEAM BUILDER, GOAL-SETTING, STARTING, REFRESHING, AND IMPROVING, VISION CASTING?

YOUR PERSONALITY

Your personality traits and how they influence your decision making and _____ with people. Two filters here:

HOW YOU _____ TO OTHERS.
- Outgoing vs Reserved
- Self-Expressive vs Self-Controlled
- Cooperative vs Competitive

HOW YOU _____ TO OPPORTUNITIES.
- High Risk vs Low Risk
- People or Projects
- Follow vs Lead
- Team vs Solo
- Routine vs Variety

A COUPLE OF GREAT RESOURCES:

Personality Assessments: No one is the end all, but using them to help provide a _____ picture will give you an insightful awareness of how you are uniquely created.
- Enneagram
- Myers Briggs
- DISC

Books:
Living Fearless by Jamie Winship

ENGAGE | CLASS TWO

EXPERIENCES

And we know that God works in all things for the good of those who love him, who have been called according to His purpose.

Romans 8:28

"Life can only be understood backwards, but it must be lived forwards."
Søren Kierkgegaard

Your past experiences are not enablers or disqualifiers, rather they are part of the story. Nothing is meant to be _____, but God uses everything to reveal, draw and encourage you and others into His love, grace and _____.

We all have experiences, _____ and _____ in several areas of our lives: personal, vocational, relational, educational & spiritual.

Through the grace and wisdom of the Holy Spirit, take some time to consider how God could _____ your positive achievements and experiences in the above categories to help shape you to who He intends you to be.

Now take some time to consider some of the negative and painful experiences in the above categories and consider how God's grace, mercy and goodness can be seen, and how He _____ you through them.

HOW DO I ENGAGE THE PURPOSE OF THE KINGDOM WHERE I LIVE?

COMMUNITY
Kingdom Presence in local community

FAMILY
Serving Opportunities

PARTNERSHIPS
Going on a trip

ENGAGE >> 127
HOW YOU'RE WIRED

NEXT STEPS

FINANCIAL PEACE UNIVERSITY

Financial Peace University is a program that has been around for decades created by Dave Ramsey. In this 9 week class you will learn how God wants us to use our financial resources, as well as practical advice on how to be wise stewards of our money. No matter where you are in your financial journey, we highly recommend taking this class.

SCAN ME!

OR VISIT: GROVE.CHURCH/FPU

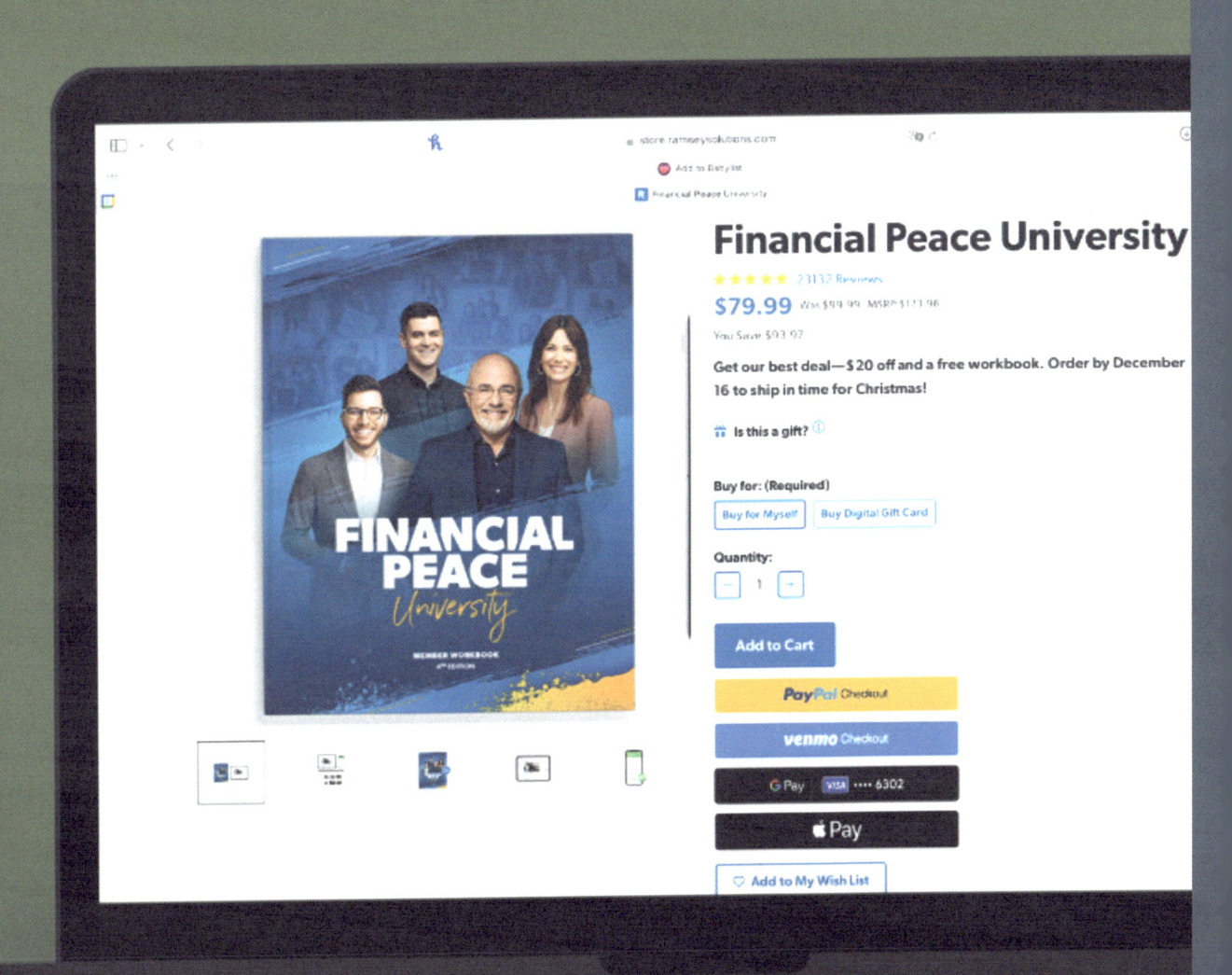

ENGAGE
FINANCIAL PEACE UNIVERSITY   >>> 129

iheart
LOVE YOUR CITY

Every year during the second week of July our church takes on dozens of projects throughout our local communities.

From painting, landscaping, throwing block parties, and creating a fun camp for kids there is a place for everyone!

We would love for you to be a part of this incredible outreach event.

Scan the QR code or visit **grove.church/iheart** for more information.

SCAN ME!

OR VISIT: GROVE.CHURCH/IHEART

SECTION THREE
LEAD 》》》

LEAD: WORKING TOGETHER TO ACCOMPLISH GOD'S MISSION

LEAD | CLASS ONE

SCAN TO SIGN UP!
OR VISIT: GROVE.CHURCH/EXPLORE-ENGAGE-LEAD-NIGHTS

THIS IS THE ~~THIRD~~ PHASE IN YOUR PATH TO CHRISTIAN MATURITY.

You've been on this journey of Exploring who The Grove Church is historically and also who we are called to be, and then jumped into the conversation of Engage, where you examined who you are, how you're wired, what it means to be on this path of a maturing Christian, and now we find ourselves in the third class of Lead.

Here we will reflect on the journey, but also look ahead. You and I were never meant to be consumers, rather, we have been called to be part of the Great Commission, and that means there is a role for you and me to play right now. In our Lead Class, we will take time to examine what this looks like.

WE HOPE YOU TAKE THIS NEXT STEP!

ARE YOU READY FOR A RECAP?

Looking back, we have spent time learning more about who The Grove Church is; it's history, vision, mission and core values.

Are you ready to review what we've learned about our church and ourselves?

RECAP OF EXPLORE
- WHO THE GROVE CHURCH IS

WHAT IS THE ONE WORD THAT DESCRIBES WHY THE GROVE CHURCH DOES WHAT WE BELIEVE GOD CALLS US TO DO?

WHAT IS THE MISSION OF THE GROVE CHURCH?

THE GROVE CHURCH CODE

We _____ up things we love for things we love even more. The church does not exist for us, we are the _____ and we exist for the world.

We are _____ people challenging real people. We are easy to be around and dedicated to growing together.

We will _____ the way with irrational generosity. We believe it is more blessed to give than to receive.

We will have Christ-centered character. We believe _____ is everything. Without it _____ else matters.

We will do anything short of _____ to reach people who don't know Christ.

We will laugh _____, hard and often. Nothing is more _____ than serving Christ with people you love.

We will _____ that we don't know everything. We will take risks, try new things, _____ and learn as we go.

We are _____ about the saving work of Jesus Christ. We know the _____ will change, but the _____ never will.

We are _____ people. We will honor God with all in, risk taking faith.

LEAD >>> 137
ACCOMPLISHING GOD'S MISSION TOGETHER

LEAD | CLASS ONE

RECAP OF ENGAGE
- USING WHO YOU ARE FOR GOD'S MISSION.

WHAT IS THE MAIN THING THAT DEFINES US?

HOW HAS GOD ENABLED YOU TO ACCOMPLISH YOUR PART IN HIS MISSION?

WHAT ARE YOUR TOP 3 SPIRITUAL GIFTS?

①

②

③

IN 1-2 SENTENCES, DESCRIBE WHAT MATURING IN CHRIST LOOKS LIKE.

WHAT ARE THE IDENTIFIERS USED TO HELP UNDERSTAND WHAT MATURING IN CHRIST LOOKS LIKE?

WHY DOES THIS MATTER?

When we _____ the mission God has given The Grove Church, and who He has created us to be, our _____ are impacted by the hope and love of Jesus! This is what Lead is all about. Leveraging the call of God for this Church and for us, His people, to fulfill the Great Commision (Matthew 28:19-20).

MEM BER SHIP

MEMBERSHIP IS A GREAT NEXT STEP IF YOU KNOW THAT THE GROVE CHURCH IS YOUR HOME CHURCH.

It's asking the question:

> "What can I do to jump in & make a difference?"

Becoming a member comes with privileges and responsibilities, all in the effort to use our unique gifts to move the mission of God forward.

After completing the Lead class, if you feel that this is the right next step, consider applying for membership.

MEMBERSHIP REQUIREMENTS:

GIVING CONSISTENTLY
Are you giving consistently to support Jesus' work through the Grove Church?

SERVING CONSISTENTLY
Are you using your gifts and talents to serve the Church body?

ACTIVELY IN COMMUNITY
Are you building deeper relationships with other people who attend the Grove? Are you plugged into consistent community?

NEXT STEPS

WHY MEMBERSHIP?

While there is no explicit statement of being a member in Scripture, the New Testament reveals the priority of being committed to a church body. (Hebrews 13:17, 1 Timothy 5:17, Hebrews 10:25).

Becoming a member shows your commitment to the local church and provides opportunities for personal leadership and growth as a follower of Jesus. As we commit to a local church it benefits our own _____, _____ and the _____

For instance: Growth into godliness can hurt. As I interact with others in my own local body, my own slothfulness in zeal is exposed, as is my lack of patience, my prayerlessness, and my hesitancy to associate with the lowly (Romans 12:11-16). Yet this interaction also gives me the opportunity to be lovingly confronted by brothers and sisters who are in the trenches with me, as well as a safe place to confess and repent.

> Membership is not just a personal or religious _____, but one of biblical _____.

SCAN TO SIGN UP!

OR VISIT: GROVE.CHURCH/MEMBERSHIP

WHAT MEMBERSHIP BRINGS

① _____

② _____

③ Expectations: _____, _____, _____

PROCESS TOWARDS MEMBERSHIP

Membership
↓
Interview
↓
Board Approval

LEAD ❯❯❯ 143
MEMBERSHIP

If you have been at our church for a while you may have been a part of giving toward the building of our new auditorium, or even the new kids wing from a few years prior.

Our next phase of our Legacy Campaign is the building of a new lobby to be able to fit everyone coming to the church.

We would love for you to prayerfully consider giving, and being a part of the miracle. You can find more information by scanning this QR code or visit **grove.church/legacy**

LEGACY
BE PART OF THE MIRACLE

SCAN ME!

OR VISIT: GROVE.CHURCH/LEGACY

NEXT STEPS

COMMIT TO THE ANNUAL BUSINESS MEETING

Everyone knows that there is nothing that sounds more exciting than a business meeting. In all seriousness these events are great opportunities to see where we are going as a church, and to celebrate all that God accomplished in the year before. When you are a member of the church you also have the opportunities to vote on multiple motions, which can be anything from confirming new board members all the way to large steps that we are taking as a church.

> If you are a member, business meeting attendance is mandatory.

However, non-members are welcome to come too and celebrate all that God is doing in our church.

MY FIRST ANNUAL BUSINESS MEETING WAS __ / __ / ____

WHAT STOOD OUT TO YOU? SHARE BELOW:

NEXT STEPS

SHARE YOUR FAITH

One of the most important truths of Christianity is that we are not meant to take our faith and keep it to ourselves. When Matthew wraps up his Gospel account, he chooses this moment where Jesus gives a command to His disciples after His resurrection:

> *Then Jesus came to them and said, "All authority in heaven and on earth has been given to me. Therefore go and make disciples of all nations, baptizing them in the name of the Father and of the Son and of the Holy Spirit, and teaching them to obey everything I have commanded you. And surely I am with you always, to the very end of the age.*
>
> (Matthew 28:18-20)

> **Jesus' command was not to just privately pursue a relationship with God, it was to make disciples!**

So for us today, this is our command. We are to help people come to know Christ, and grow in their faith. This step can be a scary one, but it's extremely important: share your faith with someone. We're not saying to grab a megaphone and hit the streets of Seattle, but rather, take inventory of your life. How many of your friends and family know that you are a Christian? Share your story of how Christ has changed your life or offer to pray for someone going through a difficult time. However you choose to do it, don't let the hope you have found in Christ just be something you keep to yourself. After you have had a chance to share your faith, take a moment to share your experience below.

SHARE YOUR EXPERIENCE BELOW:

LEAD | CLASS TWO

HOW TO LEAD

SCAN TO SIGN UP!

OR VISIT: GROVE.CHURCH/HOW-TO-LEAD

HOW DO YOU ACTUALLY LEAD?

Leadership is something that we can all know conceptually, but when it comes to practicality, the question becomes how do you actually lead?

The goal in this class is tol take a look at what leadership is, and then in turn, how we lead with those characteristics in mind, both in The Grove Church as well as in the communities and environments we are part of.

"WHAT" BEFORE "HOW"

Before we can tackle the question of how we must first understand _____ leadership is. Below is what we would call the foundational pieces to what leadership is.

Defined - the act of being a servant.

Matthew 20:26-28 - "...whoever wants to be _____ among you must be your servant...just as the Son of Man did not come to be served, but to _____..."
Romans 12:3-8 - "...not to think of himself more highly than he should think..."
Philippians 2:3-4 - "Do nothing out of selfish ambition or conceit, but in humility..."

One of the first foundational pieces to understanding leadership from a Christ-centered perspective, is that leadership is servanthood. It's not about _____, it's about _____. And because He served...we serve.

> **Leaders at The Grove Church _____ through servanthood.**

Defined - the act, state or right of possessing something.

When we talk about ownership, we are not talking as if you have a financial stake in the business endeavors of the Grove Church. We are talking about ownership in the sense that we not only understand and say yes to the vision and mission of The Grove Church, but we carry the weight as an owner would.

1 Timothy 4:12 - "...but set an example for the believers in speech, in conduct, in love, in faith and in purity."
Luke 6:31 - "Just as you want others to do for you, do the same for them."

Defined - the quality of being honest and having strong moral principles, moral uprightness; the state of being whole and undivided.

- Proverbs 10:9 - "The one who lives with integrity lives securely, but whoever perverts his ways will be found out."
- 1 Peter 2:12 - "Conduct yourselves honorably among the Gentiles, so that when they slander you as evildoers, they will observe your good works and will glorify God on the day He visits."

Integrity is more than just morality. Living with integrity means we live with the Glory of God in mind and action. Integrity is _____ for leaders at The Grove.

Defined - the ability to think about or plan the future with imagination or wisdom.

- Proverbs 11:14 - "Without vision, people perish..."
- Proverbs 16:9 - "A person's heart plan his ways, but the LORD determines his steps."
- Matthew 28:19-20 - "Go, therefore, and make disciples of all nations..."

Vision isn't just about what the lead pastor sees, it's about the Kingdom mission, and working to fulfill God's call in the church and community He has called you to be part of.

Here at The Grove, Leaders who lead with vision, not only understand and resonate with our vision, but lead in helping fulfill the Kingdom Mission to our community and the world. You're not just a follower, you are a disciple who is active in discipling others.

Defined – the capacity to have an effect on the character, development, or behavior of someone or something, or the effect itself.

- Matthew 5:14-16 - "You are the light of the world... No one lights a lamp and puts it under a basket..."
- Proverbs 27:17 - "Iron sharpens iron, and one person sharpens another."

One of the most famous definitions of leadership has influence attached to it. As a leader you have influence over others. The bigger question is how do you steward this influence.

Our greatest influence is Christ, and in turn we should lead in a way that reflects His life, love, grace, and truth above all else.

HOW TO LEAD?

Defined – the action of leading a group of people or an organization.

Leadership requires an understanding of the above, but also requires one to stay connected to Jesus and walking in humility.
- John 15:1-8 - "...Remain in me, and I in you. Just as the branch is unable to produce fruit by itself unless it remains on the vine, neither can you unless you remain in me..."

You lead effectively when you know who you are, the vision and mission of the Grove Church, and walk humbly in alignment to Christ's call for The Grove.

Practically this looks like finding your spot in the body and engaging not just in a role but leading in servanthood, ownership, integrity, vision and influence as The Holy Spirit empowers you.

WHO IS CALLED TO LEAD?

AS FOLLOWERS OF JESUS, YOU ARE CALLED TO LEAD.

"But you will receive power when the Holy Spirit has come on you, and you will be my witnesses..."

(Acts 1:8)

NEXT STEPS

JOIN A MISSIONS TEAM

This is the most expensive single next step in the whole book, but also one of the most rewarding. A missions trip is when a group of Christians travel outside of their home area (often to a foreign nation) and help with the work of the Gospel. This can be anything from working with orphans and teaching them about Jesus, building a Christian school to help serve that community, or even working with relief when a natural disaster strikes.

At the Grove we have a consistent rhythm of taking missions trips, most often to Central and South American countries. These are great opportunities to get outside of your comfort zone and grow in your faith as you serve others. If you are physically and financially able, we highly recommend that you sign up to go on one of our upcoming trips.

SCAN ME!

OR VISIT: GROVE.CHURCH/GROVE-MISSIONS

USE THIS SPACE TO WRITE ABOUT YOUR MISSIONS TRIP EXPERIENCE:

Do you feel that God may be calling you to church ministry either as a career or layperson? You may want to consider joining the Grove Church School of Ministry.

In this program you will learn the ins and outs of the way that we do ministry here at the Grove, learn from different pastors about what ministry truly looks like, and all the while earn your degree from an accredited university at an affordable price.

If this sounds like you scan the QR code or visit **grove.church/schoolofministry** for more information about the program and how to apply.

SCAN TO SIGN UP!

OR VISIT: GROVE.CHURCH/SCHOOLOFMINISTRY

SCHOOL OF MINISTRY

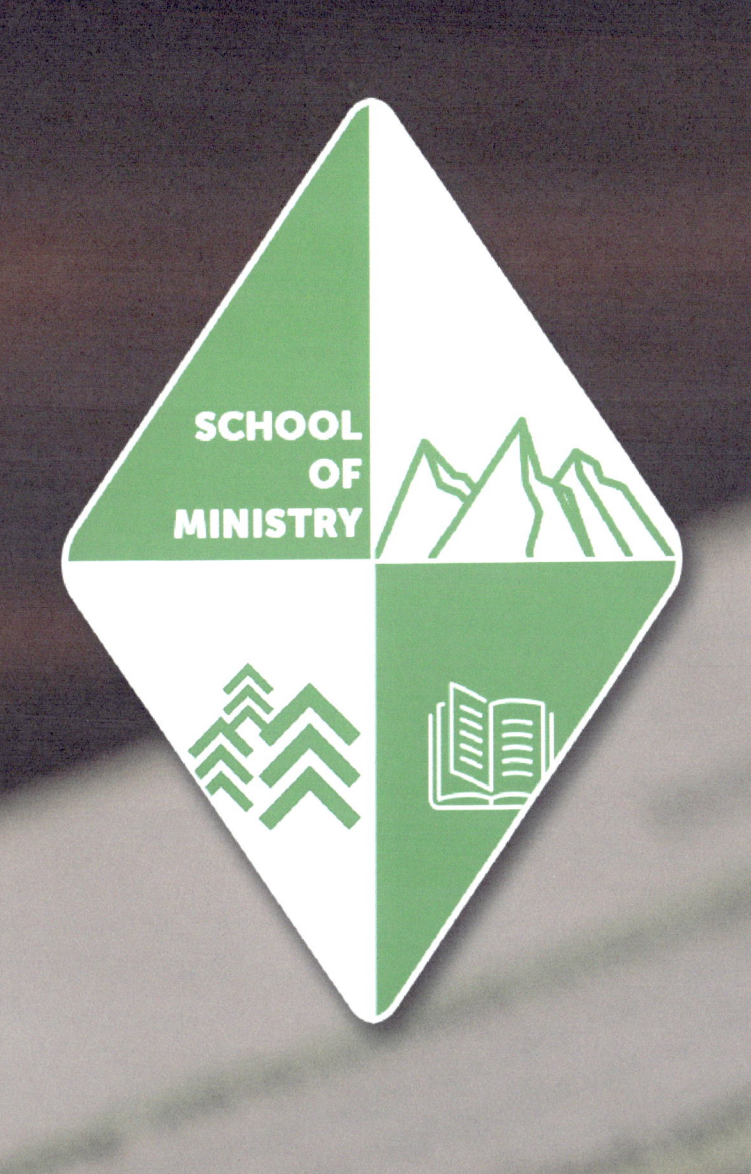

THE CODE

INTEGRITY

We will have Christ-centered character.

We believe integrity is everything. Without it, nothing else matters.

GROVE KIDS PRESENTS

BACK TO SCHOOL BASH

We know that it can be difficult to get everything together for the school year for many families in our community. So every August we throw a Back to School Bash where everyone is welcome.

We give away backpacks, water bottles, haircuts, sports physicals, and more. If you would like more information on this event, or to register to volunteer to help make it happen, scan the QR code or visit grove.church/b2sb

SCAN ME!

OR VISIT: GROVE.CHURCH/B2SB

THE CODE

REACHING

We will do anything short of sin to reach people who don't know Christ.

NOTES

Made in the USA
Columbia, SC
09 February 2025